Achieving Success as a 21st Century Manager

Achieving Success as a 21st Century Manager

Dean E. Frost

BEP

BUSINESS EXPERT PRESS

Leader in applied, concise business books

Achieving Success as a 21st Century Manager

Cover design by Charlene Kronstedt

Interior design by Exeter Premedia Services Private Ltd., Chennai, India

First published in 2021 by
Business Expert Press, LLC
222 East 46th Street, New York, NY 10017
www.businessexpertpress.com

ISBN-13: 978-1-63157-397-2 (paperback)
ISBN-13: 978-1-63157-398-9 (e-book)

Business Expert Press Human Resource Management and Organizational Behavior Collection

Collection ISSN: 1946-5637 (print)
Collection ISSN: 1946-5645 (electronic)

First edition: 2021

10 9 8 7 6 5 4 3 2 1

This book is dedicated to my wife Kathryn; she helped me make a life development plan.

Description

This book helps you take personal control of your career in management by making a custom plan for your development outside of training sessions or university degree programs. Careers and organizations are changing rapidly, so personalizing your own training and competency development is critical. Talent management is what your employer may offer to you, but action learning in the workplace means building your own managerial competencies without losing a single day on the job. Use this book to spot your best learning opportunities within your current job and then learn how you can plan your job assignments and job behaviors to build valuable, portable, and job-relevant knowledge, skills, and abilities. Included in the book are self-evaluations for cognitive competence, virtual competence, emotional competence, cross-cultural competence, socialization competence, health competence, and competencies in spotting leadership differences and situational recognition. You will find sound applied strategies in each chapter for building these competencies into strengths that will further your career in management. Every chapter contains a section on why the competency being discussed is important to your employer and why building greater levels of competency can help to make your organization more effective so that after building up your competencies you can approach the next job transition or promotional opportunity relying on your career strengths and know how to explain why they are valuable in managerial roles.

Keywords

managerial competencies; management skills; applied management development; talent management; leader development; how to lead; first-time manager

Contents

CHAPTER 1

Introduction to an Action Learning Approach to Management Development

Popular business self-help books are common that are based on anecdotes about how successful managers and business leaders operate in their work environments. Just knowing how someone else functions, especially in a specific industry or organization, which might be very different from one's own situation, is interesting but not necessarily going to lead to the reader developing new competencies. For a reader to build new competencies, what is needed is knowledge regarding how to develop management-related skills that can be transferred easily to a person's current situation or even transferred to future situations and thereby create a stronger management career. Such learning may have implications for other areas in a reader's life since they may produce healthier, satisfying, and productive relationships in nonwork areas of life as well. Ideally, these skills should be: (1) behavioral in that they describe specific actions that the individual may perform and that lead to clear outcomes, (2) controllable in the sense that they are implemented and controlled by the individual and are not the product of traits or personality attributes, and (3) developable, meaning that a person can strive to improve their performance over time (Whetton and Cameron 2011). It is important to note, however, that managers must be aware of their current levels of competency, which then helps them to be motivated to improve those levels. Most managers receive little feedback on their specific competencies from their annual reviews or from their direct supervisors. Mintzberg (1973) hoped that university-based schools might provide such feedback: "Our management schools need to identify the skills managers use, select students who show potential in these skills, put the students into situations where these skills can be practiced, and then give them systematic feedback on their performance." It is clear today, some 45 years later, that management schools have not become oriented to do these things, so university-based learning frequently fails to meet Mintzberg's standards. Self-assessment, followed by intelligent application, may be vital to continuing to develop positive competencies for career success.

In a study of 136 companies that issue initial public offerings (i.e., initial public offerings [IPOs] for startup firms), it was found that effective management of staff was judged to be the most important factor in predicting which firms survived a minimum of five years after the IPO (Welbourne and Andrews 1996). This management factor explained more of outcomes than industry, size of the firm, or profits achieved. The companies that did better at managing their people tended to survive longer. This is impressive since it is across industries and happens regardless of the size of the organization and means that management skills contribute more than just achieving profits. The reason for bringing this up here is to say that organizations, be they for-profit or nonprofit, should be strongly interested in helping managers self-assess their competencies and then to provide developmental opportunities for those managers.

Training in organizations hopes to increase individuals' capabilities to meet job demands. Training efforts range from required and regular training such as mandated by legal and administrative rules (e.g., Occupational Safety and Health Administration, Equal Employment Opportunity Commission) to technical or technologically based training (e.g., introducing a new Enterprise Resource Planning system). A common distinction is made, however, between training and development, with development usually being associated with the individual gaining new capabilities useful for both present and future jobs (Mathis and Jackson 2011). Furthermore, most employers today have managerial competency models that target desired capabilities in their managerial staff and of course they hope the competencies transfer from one job to the next.

Management development is said to be training that has both an immediate and a long-term organizational benefit (Vicere and Fulmer 1997). But these developmental efforts can be expensive and in times of economic recession, organizations may take a hard look at the disadvantages of traditional management development efforts. Most management development programs are offered as off-the-job and even off-the-job-site activities (Rothwell and Kazanas 1994). There are costs associated with developing a program or contracting with an outside training program developer. There are costs associated with paying the trainees to attend. It is expensive to pay training staff, buy training materials, and keep training records. There are even opportunity costs for decreased productivity during the times the employees are absent from their work roles.

Learning formats differ in their acceptance by trainees and their prior history of transfer of training. Table 1.1 lists six common learning formats (e.g., from formal instruction such as platform training to wilderness trips as a form of training) and some commonly discussed disadvantages to each format. This book proposes a systematic means to assess management development needs in the individual manager, which might then be linked to common on-the-job experiences which, when selectively engaged in may lead to substantial benefits in terms of targeted managerial competencies and capabilities. This type of system can be more cost-effective, can have the most face validity, and can minimize transfer of training losses, thus it may help avoid some of the disadvantages of common learning formats.

Historically, typical forms of on-the-job training included job rotation, cross-training, and apprentice training, but all of these forms are not highly relevant to management development. Other training programs such as hiring trainers to come on site, outsourcing training, and sending

Table 1.1 Disadvantages of off-site development programs

Learning format	Possible disadvantage
Formal instruction	Expense of pay trainees and trainers while off the job Requires verbal and study skills Inhibits transfer of learning
Simulation	Costly to develop the experience itself Cannot always duplicate real situations with fidelity
Assessment center	Costly to develop or to send trainees to if agency directed Takes time to administer
Role-playing	Cannot recreate true motivations from situation Role playing behaviors may not be real or transferable
Sensitivity training	May not relate to job and/or co-workers
Wilderness trips	Costly to administer Physically challenging

managers to conferences and workshops and/or educational programs require taking managers away from their current jobs, which has become too expensive for organizations. In addition, the long-term transfer of knowledge may not occur.

Studies show that investment in management development improves financial performance and that management development for the most part is self-development. Therefore, the starting point is to have a method in place that will provide the feedback essential for identifying and prioritizing management development by determining the required management competencies, assessing the manager's current capabilities, and determining how to incorporate into their current roles the experiences needed to advance to the highest level of each competency.

Managerial Competency Models

Any managerial competency model that an organization develops reflects its vision and its mission statement. Each individual manager's specific application of that model may further reflect the organization's tactical objectives related to the manager's working duties. In any case, the purpose of an organization developing a managerial competency model is to suggest that the organization has a valid idea of what they want from managerial staff and it indicates that the organization is seeking a cost-effective strategy for moving its managers further along in developing those capabilities. This book proposes that individual managers are capable of reflective self-assessments of their current work group, associated tasks, and customer focus as well as how they stand on common managerial competencies. In organizations with formalized mentorship programs, such assessments may be done with a mentor's help. This book's proposal is then to offer instruments that may be useful in that self-assessment.

Organizations may adapt or create a management competency rating form that describes a set of manager competencies. The competencies may include leadership, customer focus, team/employee development, professionalism, business knowledge, accountability, people management, and personal performance (Frost and Wallingford 2013). Each competency may have as many as five or six levels (the current example has three levels, see Table 1.2) arranged in increasing order of behavioral demands and

Table 1.2 Management competency rating form

Dimension	Description
Leadership:	Level 1: Conveys confidence in others and motivates through example. Level 2: Encourages improvement and energizes others to achieve organizational goals. Level 3: Inspires others to achieve organizational vision.
Customer focus:	Level 1: Understands customer's needs and ensures customer satisfaction. Level 2: Partners with customers to create value and improve upon customer requirements. Level 3: Seeks customer perspective to create a competitive advantage.
Team/Employee development:	Level 1: Supports employee development, assesses employee needs, and provides feedback. Level 2: Work with employees to develop a personalized developmental plan and provides long-term coaching. Level 3: Mentors others and creates long-term training goals.
Professionalism:	Level 1: Demonstrates concerns about meeting standards of performance and follows professional standards even when not in self-interest. Level 2: Models high standards of professionalism and insists upon high standards of professionalism from others. Level 3: Insists upon high standards of professionalism from the organization.
Business knowledge:	Level 1: Demonstrates business knowledge and utilizes resources to increase knowledge. Level 2: Recognizes and addresses marketplace developments and shares knowledge learned. Level 3: Foresees future trends and understands how they may impact the organization.
Accountability/Managing performance:	Level 1: Insists upon high performance and monitors progress against objectives. Level 2: Holds other accountable for their performance and takes appropriate action to address performance issues. Level 3: Takes action to hold others accountable.
People management:	Level 1: Provides direction and readily participates. Level 2: Promotes cooperation and collaboration among employees and keeps them informed. Level 3: Seeks and values input from others, learns from others, and positions self as a leader.
Personal performance:	Level 1: Works to meet organizational standards and continuously improves performance. Level 2: Develops own measures of excellence and established challenging goals. Level 3: Anticipates, takes thoughtful action, and strives for revolutionary improvement via calculated risks.

characteristic sophistication that defines a logical step-by-step development sequence. Each level builds upon the levels below it. Performance increases gradually as the competency level increases with the target competency level set at the highest level. Any effort spent developing beyond the target level would be better invested in developing a different competency. The initial competencies of all managers are determined via a management competency rating form that may be a manager's self-assessment or it may also be utilized like a 360-degree feedback method wherein the employee, co-workers, and supervisor assess all competency areas of the described manager to determine what competencies need to be the focus for future development.

Assessing current management competencies allows the described manager, in this case the reader of this book, to come up with a plan for what management development may be needed and how to implement opportunities that provide the manager with the experiences needed in order to increase competency while performing their current role. Once a management development plan is created, ongoing communication between the manager and their mentor and/or supervisor is the best way to determine the level of competency achieved and provide continued support to continue to master the highest competency level in all areas the reader deems essential. This reinforces and supports the efforts made throughout the year, modifying priorities and resources as needed. It involves continuously striving to achieve the highest level of competency and so there should be an emphasis on frequent feedback and reinforcement. This provides both formal and informal opportunities to discuss progress toward improved capabilities, review demonstration of competencies, and determine if any goals should be modified.

In applying these ideas to your own situation, the first step is to decide whether your current organization has a managerial competency model. If it does, you may want to use it in place the one presented in Table 1.2. If your current employer does not have a model like the one presented here, then you can consider using this one. If your organization, or indeed your profession, does have one you might still want to modify it to fit your future career plans. In any case, the choice is your own but be sure to be future-oriented in your planning.

At the heart of the discussion so far is the idea that management development leads to increasingly stronger managerial competencies. The next step or question to address would be whether one can actively learn the skills inherent in these managerial competencies intentionally, perhaps even speed up the process. In other words, simply occupying your role at work brings experience and with that experience comes new skills and competencies. Active learning by highlighting specific competencies and actively learning by selectively seeking out relevant experiences may speed along learning by experience.

Dragoni et al. (2009) have built a convincing argument for how linking work experiences within developmentally loaded job assignments produces strong gains for early-career managers. Managers must have access to growth assignments to achieve higher levels of competence based on the job experiences contained within the assignments. Dragoni et al. (2009) have developed a short measure of the degree of access to developmental opportunities that readers of this book can use to examine their own jobs.

Access to Highly Developmental Managerial Assignments

1. I have had access to assignments/jobs that require learning new knowledge and skills.

1	2	3	4	5
Not at all descriptive	Slightly descriptive	Moderately descriptive	Very descriptive	Extremely descriptive

2. I have had good opportunities for getting developmental assignments/jobs while working at my company.

1	2	3	4	5
Not at all descriptive	Slightly descriptive	Moderately descriptive	Very descriptive	Extremely descriptive

3. Since I have worked in this organization, I have had lots of chances to pursue challenging assignments.

1	2	3	4	5
Not at all descriptive	Slightly descriptive	Moderately descriptive	Very descriptive	Extremely descriptive

Scoring

A score between 12 and 15 is a high score indicating above average developmental opportunities. A score between 10 and 11 is an average score. A score of 9 or less indicates below average developmental opportunities. To receive the greatest benefit from reading the rest of this book your current assignment should lead to an average or higher score on this scale.

The learning described in this book goes beyond what your organization may currently provide, and it will combine elements of management development and leader development. Organizations not only invest in capital assets but also in human capital. There are four means by which organizations typically invest in human capital: (1) by contracting out functions or work to service vendors, (2) by forming strategic alliances based on complementary competitive advantages, (3) by acquiring firms for their new and valuable expertise, and (4) by developing internal assets (Lepak and Snell 1999).

In a classic study, Mintzberg (1973) found evidence that upper-level executives show consistency in their core activities. After observing managers, Mintzberg listed nine major duties or responsibilities: Supervising, Planning and Organizing, Decision Making, Monitoring Indicators, Controlling, Representing, Coordinating, Consulting, and Administering. While this seems like an exhaustive list, it contains categories that are not mutually exclusive, so it failed to lead to a universal list of managerial competencies.

Rigby (1998) studied 4,137 managers in North America, Europe, and Asia for evidence that managerial actions led to organizational success. The list of success predictors includes such factors as strategic planning, pay for performance, presence of strategic alliances, the measurement of customer satisfaction, and shareholder value analysis, and others. None of these factors help one to define how to acquire competency as a manager.

In discussing the essence of success in organizational management, Katz and Kahn (1978) noted that "the essence of organizational leadership is to be the influential increment over and above mechanical compliance with routine directions of the organization." In a similar vein, Bass (2008) felt that managers lead as a consequence of their status, meaning the power of their position in the authority hierarchy causes others to comply with their directions. What distinguished leadership from management was gaining influence over others by building perceptions of respect and esteem from others apart from one's position in the organization. This fits with Day (2001) who saw management development as different from leadership development and further that leader development as different from leadership development. Leader development is building the capabilities or competencies of the individual, whereas leadership development can be an organizational capability (i.e., the capabilities of many individuals within the organization).

Management development emphasizes specific types of knowledge, skills, and abilities that enhance the manager's task performance (Baldwin and Padgett 1994; Day 2001). Thus, management development is a set of proven solutions to known problems and is focused on performance in formal managerial roles. Leader development is for organizational roles with or without formal authority and seeks to build capacity to meet as yet unknown challenges. Mintzberg (1996) said that managers don't need to be heroes or turnaround doctors, however, noting that excellence in management can be demonstrated in everyday or noncrisis-oriented actions. Mintzberg states "a leader has a craft style of management, inspiring but not empowering, using mutual respect and drawing out the knowledge embedded in all parts of the organization." The goal of this book is to introduce the reader to those competency areas that will contribute both to the craft of management and to the development of the individual as a leader, in other words to help the reader benefit from both management development and leader development.

As of 2008, over 250,000 students study in MBA programs resulting in about 100,000 MBA degrees being awarded annually (Murray 2012). MBA degrees represent nearly 66 percent of all graduate degrees conferred by universities. This degree, while certainly costly in terms of tuition dollars and years spent in study, probably builds administrative capabilities and financial skills the best, even if it falls short in building leadership capabilities. It is a standardized, one-size-fits-all preparation that no longer sets a graduate apart from other managers. A better system will apply to both the formal roles and informal roles of management (Mabey and Thomson 2001).

Management training still needs to provide a coherent view of what managers need to learn, but delivery needs to be more flexible and fit into the busy working lives of managers ... the development of interpersonal and leadership skills is a high priority and not easily achieved through conventional formal training (Hirsh and Carter 2002).

Some have asserted that job experiences contribute more than classroom training programs to the development of senior managers (McCall, Lombardo, and Morrison 1988). Job experiences are developmental because they are opportunities to try out skills in situations that matter (McCauley et al. 1994). The types of lessons based on work experiences can be grouped into five basic themes: Agenda setting such as finding problem solution alternatives, handling of relationships, basic managerial values, executive temperament, and personal insights (i.e., self-insights). These authors feel possessing a greater background in all these areas typifies the most successful executives. Each of these themes is related to the content of this book in Table 1.3.

Table 1.3 Fundamental themes of successful management related to this book's chapters

Management theme	Chapter title
Personal insights	Introduction to an Action Learning Approach to Management Development Leadership Differences Competence Situational Recognition Competence
Agenda setting	Cognitive Competence Virtual Competence
Handling relationships	Emotional Competence
Basic values	Cross-Cultural Competence Socialization Competence
Executive temperament	Health Competence

Armstrong (2006) suggests that managers must take the main responsibility for their own development beyond formal training programs or supervisory/mentoring relationships. Managers should be able to answer the following questions:

What knowledge or skills do you intend to gain?

What levels of competence will you achieve?

What are your learning objectives and what the means to reach those objectives (e.g., tasks, projects, exercises, readings, and so on)?

What evidence will you have to demonstrate your learning?

The Principles of Action Learning

Before beginning to develop your competencies that you have targeted for development, it is relevant here to review the principles of action learning. In other words, what are the best practices in adult, continuing education that you might apply to your search for 21st century managerial competencies? The increased reliance on experiential techniques for management development is in part a recognition of the need for lifelong learning (Keys and Wolfe 1988).

Action learning is a specific orientation toward management education and development that has been practiced since the mid-1970s (Pedler, Burgoyne, and Brook 2005). It is based on adult learning principles and favors practitioner ideas in promoting transfer of training content back to workplace contexts. One such action learning model is the ALAPA learning process model (Quinn et al. 2015). Each letter in the acronym represents a step in the five-step model. See Figure 1.1 for a visualization of this ALAPA learning model.

The ALAPA learning process

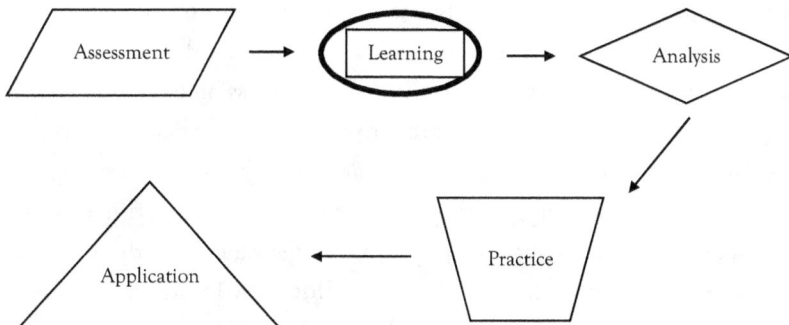

Figure 1.1 The ALAPA learning process

Assessment is the first step in the ALAPA model. Here the individual learner is seeking to discover his or her own present level of ability or knowledge and seeks to increase their self-awareness. There are many ways of making assessment accessible and valid, they range from participating in discussions, to observational systems, to role-plays, and to paper and pencil questionnaires. This book has used written scales or surveys for assessment purposes. Learning is the next step and involves reading or viewing materials on a topic. This might be texts, lectures, videos, or programmed learning materials. The third step is analysis which may determine the nature of acceptable and unacceptable behavior for a given situation. Chapter 3 in this text specifically explores some of the most common contextual elements in management and that is when we will most directly seek to match the person to the learning situation. The fourth step is practice. Practice can be simple memorization or repetition but in many instances in this book we will discuss other opportunities you may have for obtaining practice opportunities and feedback. The final step is application. In most training contexts, the principle of transfer of training means how much training content truly is implemented in the current work environment with co-workers. Since the goal of this book is to provide you with ideas and skills that build portable management competencies, much of the application may be in future tasks or jobs. We seek both short-term and long-term applications here.

Critical thinking is a meta-cognitive skill that most action learning seeks to promote in trainees. Critical thinking, according to Paul and Elder (2001), is "the disciplined art of ensuring that you use the best thinking you are capable of in any set of circumstances" (p. xiii). There are several aspects of critical thinking such as the elements of thought, levels of thought, universal intellectual standards, intellectual traits, stages of critical thinking, and a few others. This short discussion of critical thinking will focus on identifying the proper standards for critical analysis.

The standards of critical thinking are used to assess reasoning, as demonstrated in reading, writing, listening, or speaking. Primary standards include "clarity, accuracy, precision, relevance, depth, breadth, logicalness, and significance" (Paul and Elder 2001). These standards are directly applicable to students or learners who write papers and business reports, or to anyone providing feedback on such written or verbal products. Phrasing these standards in terms of useful questions, we can list the following standards.

Clarity

Is the sentence, paragraph, concept, or paper clear? Do I understand it? Would an example help me to understand? Would anything help me understand it?

Accuracy

Is this sentence, paragraph, concept, or paper true? How could the sentence, paragraph, concept, or paper be supported, justified, confirmed, or falsified?

Precision

Is this sentence, paragraph, concept, or paper precise or specific, or is it more of an abstract generality? What could make this sentence, paragraph, concept, or paper more specific and more meaningful to the reader? What details could be included to improve precision?

Relevance

Is this sentence, paragraph, concept, or paper related in some way to the topic under discussion? What improvement might be included to bring it into alignment?

Depth

Does this sentence, paragraph, concept, or paper cover the topic in sufficient depth, or does it just provide a high-level perspective that while interesting may be essentially meaningless?

Breadth

Does this sentence, paragraph, concept, or paper cover the topic in sufficient breadth, or does it just provide a narrow perspective?

Logic

Is this sentence, paragraph, concept, or paper logical and make any sense? Is there any supporting evidence? Does one element follow another or are these elements a sort of jumbled mess?

Significance

Does this sentence, paragraph, concept, or paper address the so what question? Would anyone care? Is it important to include or is it filler?

These eight universal standards are helpful in assessing sentences, paragraphs, concepts, or entire papers. The intent of discussing these standards is to improve student or learner reading, writing, listening, and speaking.

Plan of the book

Chapter 1, "Introduction to an Action Learning Approach to Management Development," outlines the book's approach to management development as a holistic assessment of person and situation. Common examples of managerial competencies are listed and explained and action learning as a perspective on skill and knowledge development is described along with the meta-cognitive skill of critical thinking.

Chapter 2, "Leadership Differences Competence," describes how management and leadership are different. The most widely used behavioral and stylistic descriptors for leadership behavior are explained and self-report measures for those descriptors are included. A discussion of four core values associated with supervising workers outlines how each manager's choice on these values may affect his or her actions in the workplace. Suggestions are included at the end of the chapter for increasing one's self-awareness of behaviors, styles, and values.

Chapter 3, "Situational Recognition Competence," asks the reader to complete measures of group atmosphere, task structure, position power, and developmental challenge. The reader can fill these out referencing their current and their anticipated future assignments. Some discussion of "situational engineering" principles for understanding how changes in personnel, tasks, or unit assignments might affect the demands made on developing manager's competencies is included in this chapter.

Chapter 4, "Cognitive Competence," begins with an explanation for the difference between perfect rationality and bounded rationality. The concepts in decision theory, which reflect managers' tendencies to use cognitive heuristics, are covered along with information on some of the most common cognitive heuristics. A means to determine how likely one is to use these cognitive heuristics is included in this chapter along with suggestions for studying how these heuristics appear in business decision-making situations and how to avoid their misuse.

Chapter 5, "Virtual Competence," discusses modern trends in leaderless groups and self-directing teams. Additionally, the challenges inherent to working over distances electronically are covered here. Assessment of the respondent's resistance to change in their working life is provided, followed by a detailed argument for why acquiring competencies in these new managerial contexts is important to organizations.

Chapter 6, "Emotional Competence," introduces the reader to emotional intelligence as a set of four skills. A self-report form for assessing one's emotional intelligence is provided with a scoring key. Why each of these four skills or capabilities is important to managerial functioning is covered in this chapter and then a set of techniques for developing greater emotional competence is presented.

Chapter 7, "Cross-Cultural Competence," refers to how societal values influence how employees function in large multinational organizations. In this chapter, a brief introduction to Project GLOBE is listed as a way of understanding how employees from cultures from around the world approach their jobs. An instrument designed for assessing the respondent's cultural preferences is contained in this chapter, followed by a discussion of why globalization affects most all organizations and of course how it affects expatriate managers. A final section shows how the reader may learn more about cultural contrasts within their own context.

Chapter 8, "Socialization Competence," deals with what has become known as onboarding in business today. The psychological and sociological implications of being a new employee or of supervising one are discussed here followed by an assessment of the reader's current organizational culture contrasted with their preferred cultural context. Next, the importance of organizational fit is discussed and approaches to understanding how best to work with employees' socialization experiences is covered.

Chapter 9, "Health Competence," talks about the concepts and processes relevant to job stressors, stress reactions, and stress coping. Two measures for stress self-assessments are in this chapter, followed by a discussion of coping systems and social support forms. The chapter ends with a reading guide for current literature on stress and coping.

CHAPTER 2

Leadership Differences Competence

What Is Competence in Recognizing Leadership Differences?

How you describe your style as a leader is an important question. One might be tempted to refer to one's personality traits and that, in fact, was the way that leadership style was described until the 1950s. Just after World War II, a very famous study published by Ralph Stogdill of Ohio State University concluded that prior evidence of a particular personality trait contributing to leadership in general had never been established (Stogdill 1948). It was at that point that many experts in the field of management followed the trend of the psychology of that era and became behaviorally oriented. In other words, at that time, they turned to describing successful management in terms of overt behaviors. A series of studies at Ohio State in the decade of the 1950s attempted to answer the question of what leaders do specifically. These studies generated a list of behaviors that leaders engaged in, both in the public sector and the private sector, and thereby produced a list of 1,800 leadership behaviors in all. Eventually, those behaviors were trimmed down to 150 specific examples and then factor analysis grouped those items into 10 factors (Fleishman 1957; Hemphill 1950).

Such an exhaustive list goes beyond our needs and in fact we want to be more basic here. We will choose to focus on two of the dimensions that those Ohio State studies produced years ago. The first is called initiating structure and the second is called consideration. What is initiating structure? Initiation includes organizing, facilitating, and sometimes resisting new ideas and practices. It may include defining and organizing work, clarifying leader versus member roles, and coordinating each direct report's tasks. Also initiating structure can include setting goals and providing incentives for the effort and productivity of employees. Consideration as a category includes things like mixing with employees, stressing on informal interactions, and engaging in personal communications. Consideration is also encouraging a pleasant atmosphere, reducing conflict, and promoting individual adjustment to the group atmosphere. Consideration can be providing information to employees, seeking information for them from them, and showing awareness of matters that affect them. Consideration can be expressing approval or disapproval of the behaviors of employees, as well as acting on behalf of the group, defending the group and advancing the interests of the group.

Initiating structure reflects the extent to which the leader defines and structures the roles of his or her direct report reports in pursuit of goal attainment. Leaders who are rated highly on initiating structure have a style that represents a more active role in directing group activities and prioritizing planning and scheduling. One way of framing the intent of the initiation structure might be to say that this is a task-oriented leadership style. The task-oriented leadership style has been characterized by Fiedler (1978) as occurring when a person whose primary goal is oriented toward task completion and whose secondary interests are in group process or the maintenance of relationships.

Consideration, on the other hand, is a leadership style that reflects the extent to which the individual creates relationships on the job characterized by mutual trust, respect for employee statements and ideas, and consideration of others' feelings. Leaders placing a strong emphasis on consideration might be described as relationship-oriented. These leaders are rated highly on creating a climate that could be characterized as showing goodwill, establishing rapport, and providing strong, two-way communication, as well as exhibiting a deep concern for the welfare of employees.

The Ohio State studies argued that initiating structure and consideration were independent concepts, meaning that the leader could be high on both, or low on both, or high on one and low on the other (Stogdill and Coons 1951). A recent meta-analysis (i.e., a mathematical analysis for confirming the results of a large number of studies on an empirical topic) of 78 studies combined the results across many organizations and many leaders (Judge, Piccolo, and Illies 2004). The meta-analysis showed that, in fact, initiating structure and consideration are only weakly related. This might be summarized as saying that knowing whether a leader engages in one style of leadership says little about whether she or he engages in the other style of leadership. This then raises the question of what style of leadership do you typically exhibit in leadership situations.

An alternative way of looking at leadership style is to attempt to address it indirectly. In this perspective, the assumption is that the individual does not easily know how to describe his or her style. In other words, you are not directly observing yourself in the same way as you would if you were observing someone else. Fred Fiedler, in his *Contingency Model of Leadership Effectiveness* (1967), proposed that identifying leadership style was best done using a projective test. This assumes, then, that the individual doesn't have an accurate ability to describe her or his own style. Fiedler created the least preferred coworker's (LPC) scale for the purposes of measuring leadership style. The LPC questionnaire itself contains sets of six of 18 contrasting adjectives, such as pleasant versus unpleasant, efficient versus inefficient, and supportive versus hostile. This scale asks the respondent to think of all the co-workers they have ever worked with and to describe the one person that they least enjoyed working with by rating that person based on their memory of that person using a scale of 1 to 8 for each of the 16 sets of contrasting adjectives. Fiedler believes that based on the respondent's answers to this LPC scale, he can determine their basic leadership style. If the least preferred co-worker is described in relatively positive terms, that is a relatively high LPC score, then the respondent is primarily interested in good personal relations within the work environment. If you essentially describe the person you are least able to work with in relatively favorable terms, Fiedler labels your style as relationship-oriented as a leader. In contrast if the least preferred co-worker is seen in relatively unfavorable terms, a relatively low LPC score, the respondent is primarily interested productivity and thus would be labeled task-oriented. About 16 percent of the respondents score in the middle of this scale. Such individuals cannot be classified as either relationship-oriented or task-oriented from their projective test results. This might represent a failure of the projective test to identify their dominant style or one might be that they are individuals describing themselves as having elements of both styles, in other words a high-high combination of both relationship-oriented and task-oriented styles. Note that Fiedler further assumes that an individual's leadership style is fixed and doesn't change over time.

Leadership is not the same as management (cf. Bass 1990). This distinction can be based on a conceptual argument or an empirical one. Conceptually, leadership is the social influence process of one person affecting the behaviors, attitudes, and values in a desired direction. Management is that and more. Management includes all the technical or task-relevant content of your job as well as the administrative work required by your organization. We concentrate on leadership and leadership style for the remainder of this chapter because that is the portable aspect of management. To achieve a truly boundaryless career, you will want to develop skills that can be transferred from organization or employer to another or even from one industry to another. Focusing on leadership, and leadership development, in this particular chapter makes sense in light of that goal.

How Are Leadership Differences Assessed?

Use the following two measures to explore your personal style as a leader. Each measure produces a similar result, but it does so in radically different ways, reflecting different assumptions about your own self-awareness. The first scale a self-report version of the Leadership Behavior Description Questionnaire adapted to describing one's idea of ideal leader behavior (Fleischman, 1957) which has become known as the Leadership Opinion Questionnaire.

Leadership Opinion Questionnaire: A good manager…

1. Refuses to give in when people disagree with what the manager has said.

0	1	2	3	4
Always	Often	Occasionally	Seldom	Never

2. Encourages overtime work.

4	3	2	1	0
A Great Deal	Fairly Much	To Some Degree	Comparatively Little	Not at all

3. Expresses appreciation when others do a good job.

4	3	2	1	0
Always	Often	Occasionally	Seldom	Never

4. Tries out new ideas the manager has thought of for a task or situation.

4	3	2	1	0
Always	Often	Occasionally	Seldom	Never

5. Is easy to understand.

4	3	2	1	0
Always	Often	Occasionally	Seldom	Never

6. Rules with an iron hand.

4	3	2	1	0
Always	Often	Occasionally	Seldom	Never

7. Makes those with less authority feel at ease when talking with him/her.

4	3	2	1	0
Always	Often	Occasionally	Seldom	Never

8. Criticizes poor work.

4	3	2	1	0
Always	Often	Occasionally	Seldom	Never

9. Sees that a direct report is rewarded for job well done.

4	3	2	1	0
Always	Often	Occasionally	Seldom	Never

10. Talks about how much should be done.

4	3	2	1	0
A Great Deal	Fairly Much	To Some Degree	Comparatively Little	Not at all

11. Rejects suggestions for changes.

0	1	2	3	4
Always	Often	Occasionally	Seldom	Never

12. Encourages slow working co-workers to greater effort.

4	3	2	1	0
Always	Often	Occasionally	Seldom	Never

13. Changes the duties of people under him without first talking it over with them.

0	1	2	3	4
Always	Often	Occasionally	Seldom	Never

14. Waits for others to push new ideas before he does.

0	1	2	3	4
Always	Often	Occasionally	Seldom	Never

15. Treats other people with less authority without considering their feelings.

0	1	2	3	4
Always	Often	Occasionally	Seldom	Never

16. Assigns people to particular tasks.

4	3	2	1	0
Always	Often	Occasionally	Seldom	Never

17. Tries to keep direct reports in good standing with those higher in authority.

4	3	2	1	0
Always	Often	Occasionally	Seldom	Never

18. Asks for sacrifices from direct reports for the good of the entire department.

4	3	2	1	0
Always	Often	Occasionally	Seldom	Never

19. Resists changes in ways of doing things.

0	1	2	3	4
Always	Often	Occasionally	Seldom	Never

20. Insists that direct reports follow standard ways of doing things in every detail.

4	3	2	1	0
Always	Often	Occasionally	Seldom	Never

21. Refuses to explain his/her own actions.

0	1	2	3	4
Always	Often	Occasionally	Seldom	Never

22. Sees to it that people with less authority are working up to their limits.

4	3	2	1	0
Always	Often	Occasionally	Seldom	Never

23. Acts without consulting direct reports first.

0	1	2	3	4
Always	Often	Occasionally	Seldom	Never

24. Offers new approaches to problems.

4	3	2	1	0
Always	Often	Occasionally	Seldom	Never

25. Backs up direct reports in their actions.

4	3	2	1	0
Always	Often	Occasionally	Seldom	Never

26. Insists that he/she be informed of any decisions made by direct reports.

4	3	2	1	0
Always	Often	Occasionally	Seldom	Never

27. Is slow to accept new ideas.

0	1	2	3	4
Always	Often	Occasionally	Seldom	Never

28. Lets others do their work the way they think best.

0	1	2	3	4
Always	Often	Occasionally	Seldom	Never

29. Treats others as his/her equal.

4	3	2	1	0
Always	Often	Occasionally	Seldom	Never

30. Stresses being ahead of competing work groups.

4	3	2	1	0
A Great Deal	Fairly Much	To Some Degree	Comparatively Little	Not at all

31. Is willing to make changes.

4	3	2	1	0
Always	Often	Occasionally	Seldom	Never

32. "Needles" direct reports for greater effort.

4	3	2	1	0
A Great Deal	Fairly Much	To Some Degree	Comparatively Little	Not at all

33. Is friendly and can be easily approached?

4	3	2	1	0
Always	Often	Occasionally	Seldom	Never

34. Decides in detail what shall be done and how it shall be done.

4	3	2	1	0
Always	Often	Occasionally	Seldom	Never

35. Puts suggestions that are made by direct reports into operation.

4	3	2	1	0
Always	Often	Occasionally	Seldom	Never

36. Emphasizes meeting deadlines.

4	3	2	1	0
A Great Deal	Fairly Much	To Some Degree	Comparatively Little	Not at all

37. Gets approval of direct reports on important matters before going ahead.

4	3	2	1	0
Always	Often	Occasionally	Seldom	Never

38. Asks other managers who have slow groups to get more out of their groups.

4	3	2	1	0
Always	Often	Occasionally	Seldom	Never

39. Criticizes a specific act rather than a particular individual.

4	3	2	1	0
Always	Often	Occasionally	Seldom	Never

40. Emphasizes the quantity of work being done.

4	3	2	1	0
A Great Deal	Fairly Much	To Some Degree	Comparatively Little	Not at all

Scoring

Sum scores on all odd-numbered items. That score represents Consideration.
Sum scores on all even-numbered items. That score represents Initiation of Structure or Structuring.
Whichever score is higher would then be your best description as a leader.

Least Preferred Co-worker Scale

Instructions:

Think of all the different people with whom you have ever worked ... in jobs, in social clubs, in student projects, or whatever. Next think of the *one person* with whom you could work least well, that is, the person with whom you had the most difficulty getting a job done. This is the one person (a peer, boss, or subordinate) with whom you would least want to work. Describe this person by circling numbers at the appropriate points on each of the following pairs of bipolar adjectives. Work rapidly. There are no right or wrong answers.

Pleasant	8	7	6	5	4	3	2	1	Unpleasant
Friendly	8	7	6	5	4	3	2	1	Unfriendly
Rejecting	1	2	3	4	5	6	7	8	Accepting
Tense	1	2	3	4	5	6	7	8	Relaxed
Distant	1	2	3	4	5	6	7	8	Close
Cold	1	2	3	4	5	6	7	8	Warm
Supportive	8	7	6	5	4	3	2	1	Hostile
Boring	1	2	3	4	5	6	7	8	Interesting
Quarrelsome	1	2	3	4	5	6	7	8	Harmonious
Gloomy	1	2	3	4	5	6	7	8	Cheerful
Open	8	7	6	5	4	3	2	1	Guarded
Backbiting	1	2	3	4	5	6	7	8	Loyal
Untrustworthy	1	2	3	4	5	6	7	8	Trustworthy
Considerate	8	7	6	5	4	3	2	1	Inconsiderate
Nasty	1	2	3	4	5	6	7	8	Nice
Agreeable	8	7	6	5	4	3	2	1	Disagreeable
Insincere	1	2	3	4	5	6	7	8	Sincere
Kind	8	7	6	5	4	3	2	1	Unkind

Scoring

Compute your LPC score by totaling all the numbers you circled. Enter that score below:

LPC = _____

Score Interpretation. The LPC scale is used by Fiedler to identify a person's dominant leadership style (Fiedler, Chemers, and Mahar 1976). Fiedler believes that this style is a relatively fixed part of one's personality and is therefore difficult to change. This leads Fiedler to his contingency views, which suggest that the key to leadership success is finding (or creating) good "matches" between style and situation. If your score is 73 or above, you are considered a "relationship-oriented" leader. If your score is 64 or below, you are considered a "task-oriented" leader. If your score between 65 and 72, you are a mixture of both, and it is up to you to determine which leadership style is most like yours.

Why Are Leadership Differences Important in Organizations?

One of the most popular psychological theories of the last two generations is Maslow's need hierarchy (Maslow 1954). This theory was the first theory to explain typical or well-adjusted adult motivation in systematic psychological ways. Maslow made three assumptions about us: First, he assumed that we had predominant or prepotent need that drives our current behavior. Second, he assumed that a satisfied need would no longer motivate a person and that a person would move on to focus on other needs in that case. Finally, he assumed that all of us potentially would strive to discover all of our abilities as completely as possible. Figure 2.1 is an illustration of his five needs arranged in a hierarchy.

The most fundamental needs or first to be addressed are at the base of the figure and in terms of work lives means striving for wages and benefits. The next most fundamental needs are safety and security needs, meaning a concern for job security and safe working conditions. The next would be social needs on the job illustrated by co-workers as friends, then esteem needs such as recognition for superior work performance and then self-actualization meaning work that is ultimately challenging and developing of all one's attributes, skills, and values.

A good way to look at leadership style is to think of it as a need hierarchy relevant to task performing groups. Some leaders have a prepotent need for task completion, but when that need is satisfied they move to being driven by the need for positive group relations. We call those leaders task-oriented or say they are exhibiting substantial Initiation of Structure behaviors. Some leaders have a prepotent need for good group atmospheres but when that need is achieved they move to being driven by the need for task completion. We call those leaders relationship-oriented or say they are exhibiting substantial Consideration behaviors. So in effect, the most obvious aspects of your leadership style are function

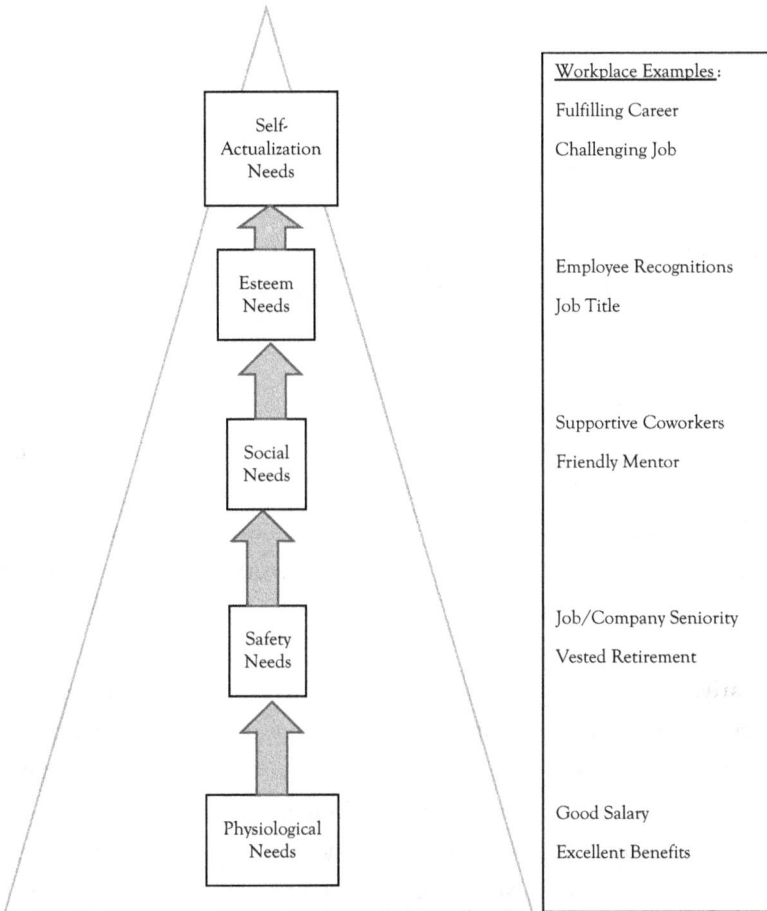

Figure 2.1 Maslow's need hierarchy

Note: Author created.

of you plus of the current situation and its recent history. Of course, it is possible to be evenly balanced with high emphasis on both goals or to have low emphasis on both goals, but people falling into those categories are relatively rare. The important message here is to use Maslow's concept of the hierarchy of needs by applying it to mean that we are all hoping and working toward important group outcomes or goals when we are managing other people.

Besides using our two measures of leadership style and the concepts from Maslow's need hierarchy, we should also recognize our own assumptions about our co-workers. I categorize these assumptions as answers to four primary questions about the four core values regarding change in humans that each of us holds to be true.

The first question is "How much change is a human capable of?" If you believe that co-workers are expressing only preexisting traits or previously learned skills, you will tend to be leader that expresses feedback only in terms of achievement of outcomes. On the other extreme, if you see co-workers as consistently striving to change and grow then you will be leader that expresses feedback in terms of the co-worker's process or progress in adapting and getting better.

The second question is "What is the capacity for learning in a human?" At one extreme, we tend to use computers for a metaphor for human functioning and often speak of using memory stores or processing data. This metaphor, however, implies limits on thinking and reasoning just as your computer has limits. One might, on the other hand, see humanity as having unlimited potential and speak of learning as if it were a tree growing up and out, as learning being a constant branching and reaching. Clearly, leaders who assign new tasks or situations to co-workers might portray these assignments differently given two such extreme orientations.

A third question is "Do internal or external factors control human behavior?" These assumptions are obvious in our reliance on extrinsic versus intrinsic factors in motivation and learning. A manager who is attentive first to the co-worker's expressed interests and values is likely to see internal drives as important to manage and direct whereas a manager who stresses the consequences of actions as altering future behavior is more likely to stress contingencies of co-workers' behaviors in seeking to be a good manager.

A fourth question is "How much proactive, assertive behavior is possible?" This similar to the internal versus external question but it relates to the initiation of behavior more than the control of ongoing behavior. What spurs us to action and gets us going in the morning upon arrival to work? Are your co-workers mainly passive and reactive or do they tend to seek out and become attracted to behaviors, whether those behaviors are beneficial or not?

Try answer each of these four questions for yourself. Next, try answering them for your current employer or organization as a whole. If there are areas that are not clear, that is OK; focus on the answers that are obvious. Values are very basic and are hard to change, so changing your values is outside of the scope of this book, but whether your values match those of current employer may lead you think of bout your person-to-organization fit. These ideas will become relevant again in Chapter 8 on Socialization Competence.

There is a strong tendency to describe others by their personal traits. The fundamental attribution error (Heider 1958) is a commonly taught principle in social psychology. This principle says that observers have a strong tendency to rely on personal characteristics in explaining why a person being observed acts the way they do (Jones and Nisbett 1987). Joe Biden, as U.S. president, is said to be empathetic whereas Vladimir Putin, as Russian president, is said to be manipulative. Historical figures like Winston Churchill are thought of as brave whereas Napoleon Bonaparte is thought to have been grandiose. Even popular business leaders are often described as possessing distinctive traits: Steve Jobs of Apple Inc. was iconoclastic and bold, but Bill Gates of Microsoft Inc. is analytical and generous. It is reasonable to assume, therefore, that others will observe you by your personal characteristics or behaviors. Psychologists tell us that the fundamental attribution error is a type of figure-ground perception. Because others are focused on us as a focal point, the elements of the situation (i.e., our job duties, our co-workers, the task at hand, and the organizational culture we work within) are a background that receives less of our attention. In sum, across many business applications, the difference between actors' attributions and observers' attributions can be summarized as actors tend to report situational factors as being most important and observers tend to report personal qualities of the person observed as being most important in explaining their outcomes. Although we cannot prevent such perceptions about us, there is value in understanding how observers in general rely on leader behaviors or stylistic elements in describing managers so that we can at least anticipate how we will be perceived as managers.

If one looks over the scholarly literature on management or leadership characteristics and how those might explain performance or effectiveness, such qualities as ambition, honesty and integrity, energy, tenacity, initiative, and self-confidence get mentioned frequently (Kirkpatrick and

Locke 1991). But it is clear that none of these trait explanations are predictive in every management role or that all successful managers demonstrate all of these traits. What does occur in most situations and by most leaders are the leader behaviors of structuring and consideration, along with behaviors encouraging participation and encouraging productivity. Zaccaro, Foti, and Kenny (1991) varied group task cues and measured experimental participants' execution of these types of leader behaviors and their data analysis found that 59 percent of the variance in ratings of leadership emergence (i.e., who becomes a group leader in a group without a designated leader) was predicted by structuring, consideration, persuasion emphasis and productivity emphasis behaviors, and task characteristics. In other words, showing structuring behaviors when the group's tasks are unstructured causes that actor to be seen as the group's new leader. However, predicting how effective the group will be or even how effective the group's leader is in facilitating task performance may be more complicated. Now this is not to discount the aforementioned trait list, but it has been argued that traits and behaviors predict the perception of who the group's leader will be better than they distinguish between effective and ineffective leaders (Lord, DeVader, and Alliger 1986).

Understanding why traits and behaviors are important attributions of leadership or management effectiveness may require identifying relevant situational or contextual factors that operate in the manager's job. For example, Steve Jobs was iconoclastic and bold, but that mattered most when he was rehired by Apple Inc. in the 1990s after their market share dropped plus it mattered greatly that touch screen technologies were just becoming feasible at that time. Moreover, Bill Gates was analytical and generous, but what mattered most was that Microsoft Inc. convinced personal computer manufacturers in the 1990s to sell their PCs with the Windows operating system preloaded with the Microsoft Office Suite. The technology that mattered in that case was the software integration in Office that allowed easy movement of data from Excel to Word to Power-Point. Microsoft was generous in loading their Office Suite onto new PCs but analytical in correctly judging that it would to their software becoming very dominant. To further understand how leadership behaviors and leadership styles matter in leadership effectiveness, we can look to the early development of contingency approaches to understanding leadership.

An early attempt to integrate both personal and situational factors into one theory was Fiedler's (1967) theory of leadership effectiveness, which become known as the contingency model of leadership. Fiedler used the Least Preferred Co-Worker Scale to measure leadership styles and plotted leadership jobs or roles on something he called situational favorability, a mix of group atmosphere, task qualities, and formal power measures. He found empirical evidence to support the ideas that relationship-oriented styles predicted greater leadership effectiveness in moderately favorable situations, but task-oriented styles predicted greater leadership effectiveness in either low favorability situations or high favorability situations. This model based on personal attributions plus situational attributions became very popular in management textbooks. Hersey and Blanchard (1974) developed another contingency approach that became very popular. They too used leadership style but the situational factor they emphasized was follower readiness. One prediction they made was that followers who were overmatched by their task demands or that were unmotivated to complete their tasks would respond best to directive styles (e.g., structuring behaviors by the leader). A second prediction was that when followers had higher task-relevant skills and/or were more motivated by their tasks would respond best to supportive, participative styles (e.g., consideration behaviors performed by the leader). A third example of a contingency approach would be the Leader–Member Exchange (LMX) Theory of Leadership (Graen and Uhl-Bien 1995). In this case, the dyadic or one-on-one interactions between the group leader and each group member result in some group members falling into an in-group and other associating with an out-group. Interactions with the in-group members and the group leader are more frequent, less formal, more trusting, and consequently lead to more mutually agreed upon or accepted assigned roles (i.e., role making supervision typified as consideration by the leader), but in turn interactions with the out-group would be less frequent, more formal, less trusting, and therefore closely supervised (i.e., role taking supervision typified by structuring leader behaviors). In all these contingency examples, there is this matching of personal attributes of the manager to the attributes of the management situation.

A fourth contingency approach called a path-goal theory of leadership effectiveness (House 1971) is worth looking at more closely here. This example is relevant to our purposes since it uses the Leadership Opinion Questionnaire labels for leader behaviors directly and then applies them to elements of the expectancy theory of work motivation (Vroom 1964). This theory of work motivation sees three critical elements in the workers' subjective perception as the effort to performance judgment (i.e., expectancy), the performance to outcomes judgment (i.e., instrumentality), and the value for outcomes judgments (i.e., valence). The theory states that to be successful the leader must provide the needed information, support, and resources to clarify the path and ensure goal attainment and subsequent rewards. Those leader behaviors are directive (e.g., structuring), supportive (e.g., consideration), achievement-oriented, and participative. The situational factors are grouped as environmental factors (e.g., elements of the group's tasks, the formal authority system, and characteristics of the primary work group) or they are grouped as subordinates' characteristics (e.g., their locus of control, their authoritarianism, and their self-perceived ability levels). The path-goal theory predicts that directive leaders will have more satisfied and more productive groups when the group's tasks are ambiguous, there is lack of clear standard policies and procedures provided by the organization, and when the group members show more authoritarian acceptance attitudes. The theory predicts that supportive leaders will be more successful if their group has structured but stressful, frustrating, or dissatisfying tasks. The theory predicts subordinates with more internal loci of control that work on ambiguous, nonrepetitive tasks will respond best to achievement-oriented leader behaviors and that subordinates that need more clarity in how their work will lead to outcomes or when subordinates have choice to exercise in which goals to pursue (i.e., greater autonomy) will respond best to participative leader behaviors.

The path-goal theory is deductively derived from the expectancy theory and from the leadership behaviors identified by the Ohio State Leadership Studies. Empirical studies of the theory have largely focused on the directive and supportive leadership behaviors previously discussed in this chapter (House 1996; Schriesheim and Neider 1996). The results have been supportive for the predictions of how directive or structuring behaviors operate in task-performing groups, both in predicting group members' ratings of satisfaction with leadership provided and with their evaluation of the leaders' effectiveness. Conclusions about supportive or consideration behaviors and leadership effectiveness are less supportive of the theory. If data for consideration behaviors and ratings of satisfaction are examined, it seems that these leader behaviors are associated with greater satisfaction across all situations. The final takeaway from this discussion of the importance of leadership differences is that whether one uses structuring and consideration behaviors as the personal attribute or one relies on task-oriented and relationship-oriented leadership styles as the personal attribute, it is very important to be aware of how others view you as a leader and a manager. Being aware of the actor-observer difference will help you to understand how participants versus observers react to workplace episodes differently and why those differences exist. Finally, our brief description of contingency approaches to leadership and to the path-goal theory leads us to see how important it is to learn how to judge situational factors systematically. That situational recognition competency is what the next chapter is about.

Where Can Competence in Recognizing Leadership Differences Be Developed?

The following are suggestions for further exploration of your leadership style. First, meet with a mentor and ask them to complete the forms from this chapter about you (i.e., as if they were you). Then compare your responses to their responses for you. You can then discuss the accuracy of the assessments and their implications. Second, you can keep a journal in which you record your workplace actions and the situations or contexts for those actions. Use these entries to help you understand your action tendencies and motivations in leadership situations. For those entries that seem most descriptive of you, go back later and try to create entries as a manager with a substantially different style or set of actions from your own. Use these alternate responses to understand your own. Third, select a manager with a very different style from your own. Take notes on the specific actions that individual makes in meeting their own job demands and record what consequences arise from their responses. Note how different or similar the sequences are to your own.

CHAPTER 3

Situational Recognition Competence

What Is Competence in Recognizing Situational Differences?

Describing in your own words your current working group might be done in a number of ways, but if we look at group dynamics research, there are three common ways that an individual workgroup is distinguished (Shaw 1981). First, we might describe the group's social atmosphere. Second, we might describe qualities of the workgroup's tasks. And third, we might describe the power and status systems operating within the group. A fourth factor is a little bit larger than the individual workgroup—the organizational culture, which we will consider later (Frost et al. 1991).

First, workgroups differ in what is called group atmosphere (Mannix and Neale 2005). Teamwork processes referred to the interpersonal activities that facilitate accomplishment of the team's work but do not directly involve task accomplishment itself. For example, transition processes are activities that focus on preparation for future work. One transition process might be strategy formulation, referring to the development of the courses of action or contingency plans. Contingency plans for how resources are to be made available to the team or activities involved in decoding the team's overall mission beyond specific and immediate tasks would be examples of transition processes. Indeed, action processes involving how the group monitors its progress toward goal might help the group with its coordination and integration of the efforts of individuals and could be a part of that group's atmosphere.

When discussing group atmosphere, probably the single most important way we can distinguish between teams is to talk about interpersonal processes. Interpersonal processes include motivating and confidence building, as well as emotional management engaged in by team members. Another important component of interpersonal processes might be conflict management. Relationship conflict refers to disagreements among team members in terms of interpersonal relationships or incompatibilities with respect to personal values and preferences. This type of conflict centers on issues that are not directly connected to the team tasks. Relationship conflict is not only dissatisfying to most people, but it also tends to reduce team performance. Task conflict, in contrast, refers to disagreements among members about the team's task. Logically speaking, this type of conflict can be beneficial to teams because it stimulates conversation and may result in the expression of new ideas and development of new group processes. Still, it is in the nature of the interpersonal interactions between group members and between the group and the group leader that best captures the concept of group atmosphere.

Groups also differ on the nature of their tasks and goals. Task interdependence refers to the degree to which team members interact with and rely on other team members for information, materials, and resources needed to accomplish work for the team. There are four primary ways that task interdependence is described by experts. The first type of task interdependence is called pooled interdependence and represents the lowest degree of required coordination. In this type of interdependence, group members complete their work and assignments independently and then the group simply sums or put together all of the group members' efforts to represent the group output. Pooled interdependence would be like fishing on a boat. Each person would bait their hooks, drop the baited line in the water, play out their lines, reel in their lines after a fish bites at the hook, remove the fish from the hook, and finally throw the fish into a tank filled with ice and other fish. At the end of the day, the boat's production would be the total weight of fish that were caught.

The second type of task interdependence is called sequential interdependence. In this type of interdependence, different tasks are done in a prescribed order, and the group is structured such that members specialize in these tasks. Although members in groups of six have independence in how they carry out their individual parts of the work, the interaction occurs only between members who perform tasks that are next to each other in the sequence. Moreover, the members performing the tasks in the latter part of the sequence depend on members performing the task. Returning to our fishing boat metaphor, each of the six steps could be performed by a different group member (i.e., one person baits the hooks, another person is responsible for dropping all the lines into the water, and so on) such that you have six separate steps in a sequence, with each step performed by a specialist. The classic assembly-line manufacturing context provides an excellent image of this type of interdependence, especially as implemented in the Rouge River plant built by Henry Ford.

Reciprocal interdependence is a third type of task interdependence. Similar to sequenced interdependence, members are specialized in performing specific tasks, but instead of the strict sequence of activities, members interact with a subset of other members to complete tasks. To understand reciprocal interdependence, think of a team of people involved in a business that sells fresh fish to retail clients (e.g., seafood restaurants). After meeting with the client, the salesperson would provide general criteria for the catch needed on a particular day, a boat captain would select the appropriate lake and trolling area, the anglers would collectively decide on proper lines and hooks and depths to troll, and someone in the group would ensure that only the right varieties of fish were caught and that the catch met the specified size requirements.

The final and fourth type of task interdependence is called comprehensive interdependence. This requires the highest level of interaction coordination among members as they try to accomplish work. In groups that display comprehensive interdependence, each member has a great deal of discretion in terms of what they do and with whom they interact in the course of collaboration to accomplish the team's work. This might be stretching the fishing metaphor, but here the best example might be a charter boat crew fishing for a prize marlin.

In addition to being linked to one another by task activities, group members might be linked by their goal interdependence. A very high degree of goal interdependence exists when team members have a shared vision of the team's goals and align their individual goals to those team goals. Outcome interdependence exists when team members must share the rewards that the team earns, so in this case reward examples including pay, bonuses, informal feedback, and recognition, as well as informal recognition, all are based on team achievement and not on an individual's goal attainments. Because team achievement depends on the performance of each team member, high outcome interdependence also implies the team members depend on the performance of other team members for the rewards they receive. In contrast, low outcome interdependence exists in teams in which individual members receive rewards and punishments on the basis of their own performance, without regard for the performance of the team.

Organizational power derives primarily from one's position within the organization especially as defined by formal organization lines of authority. This type of legitimate power derives from a position of authority inside the organization and usually is related to possessing some sort of job title, or a place in an organizational chart, or even a title on one's office door. Those with legitimate power have the understood right to ask others to do things that are considered within the scope of their job assignments. When managers ask direct reports to stay late to work on a project, to work on one task instead of moving on to a second task, or to work faster, they are exercising legitimate power. Generally speaking, the higher up in an organization a manager rises, the more legitimate power they possess because of their position. Related to this type of legitimate control is the right to reward and punish direct reports. Reward power exists when a manager has control over resources are rewards that a direct report might desire as a reward. This might be the ability to recommend a promotion or a bonus or even to give time off. Awarding punishments and the ability to recommend or control the delivery of undesired consequences in an organization also is related one's position as a manager. A manager might have the right to fire, demote, suspend, or lower the pay of an employee or to recommend such actions.

To summarize the key situational factors in describing differences between work groups, one can rely on group atmosphere, task structure, and position power. Group atmosphere is the degree of confidence, trust, and respect members have in their leader in their group leader and among themselves as members of the group. Task structure is the degree to which job assignments or procedure are structured or unstructured relative by instruction or by evaluation. Position power is the degree of influence a leader has over power variables such as hiring, firing, discipline, promotions, and salary increases.

How Are Situational Differences Assessed?

Situational determinants of leadership effectiveness are commonly used in both theory and practice in management. The contingency model of leadership effectiveness (Fiedler, 1978), the path-goal theory (House and Mitchell, 1974), and the substitutes for leadership model (Kerr and Jermier 1978) all explicitly discuss how important the task structure of a group's primary tasks is to understand how effective leadership may be within the group. This book proposes that all managers should periodically examine their task structure and consider how changes in their own work routines or in organizational policies may impact that dimension (see Table 3.1).

An excellent self-assessment form is given in Fiedler, Chemers, and Mahar (1976). This 10-item rating form is easily completed by any manager in minutes and describes the four primary dimensions of task structure. The four dimensions are Decision Verifiability (e.g., the degree to which the correctness of a solution or a decision can be demonstrated), Goal Clarity (e.g., the degree to which duties and related outcomes are clearly understood), Goal Path Multiplicity (e.g., the degree to which there exists more than one set of procedures for approaching work on the task), and Solution Specificity (e.g., the degree to which there exists more

Table 3.1 Examples of task characteristics

Task characteristic	Example
Job description	Objectives Activities Equipment or tools Inputs: Information, materials, component tasks
Workload	Time or cognitive demand
Workflow	Central to others' tasks or Independent
Communication media	Face-to-face, e-mail, logs
Working conditions	Shop floor, retail environment, office
Task interrelationships	Complete task identity to individual component
Technology	Machine mediated to expert judgment only
Task structure	Solution Specificity Goal Path Multiplicity Feedback
Performance measurement	Subjective rating to quantitative index

than one correct outcome to work on the task). High scores on task structure make a manager's job relatively easier, but even when a manager sees her or his job as highly structured, examining the tasks again may suggest ways of de-structuring the tasks in ways that are useful. Such might be the case when managers voluntarily take on new tasks, especially difficult unresolved problems, or seek to produce greater creativity or innovation in the organization.

Task Structure Rating Form

1. Is there a standard operating procedure (SOP), a diagram, or a detailed description that explains how to do the tasks that make up your job?

   2=Usually True   1=Sometimes True   0=Seldom True

2. Is there a person available to advise you on how the job should be done?

   2=Usually True   1=Sometimes True   0=Seldom True

3. Is there a step-by-step or by-the-numbers procedure which explains in detail how to do the task that make up your job?

   2=Usually True   1=Sometimes True   0=Seldom True

4. Is there a way to divide the task into separate parts or steps?

   2=Usually True   1=Sometimes True   0=Seldom True

5. Are there some ways which are clearly recognized as better than others for doing your job?

   2=Usually True   1=Sometimes True   0=Seldom True

6. Is it obvious when a task in your job is finished?

   2=Usually True   1=Sometimes True   0=Seldom True

7. Is there a book, a manual, or a job description, which indicates the best solution or the best outcome for each task in your job?

   2=Usually True   1=Sometimes True   0=Seldom True

8. Is there a general understanding about the standards you have to meet for your work to be considered acceptable?

   2=Usually True   1=Sometimes True   0=Seldom True

9. Are you usually given a numerical rating on how well you did your job?

2=Usually True   1=Sometimes True   0=Seldom True

10. Can you find out how well a task in your job has been done in enough time to be able to do it the next time?

2=Usually True   1=Sometimes True   0=Seldom True

Scoring

Sum responses to all items for your task structure score.

Another dimension that management jobs vary on is the degree to which they endow the manager with social bases for power. Fiedler, Chemers, and Mahar (1976) developed a self-report measure for positional power. Use the following scale to assess your power given your current job title and current employer.

Position Power Rating Form

1. Can you directly or by recommendation administer rewards and punishments to your direct reports?

2	1	0
Can Act Directly Or Recommend With High Effectiveness	Can Recommend but With Mixed Results	No

2. Can you directly or by recommendation affect the promotion, demotion, hiring, or firing of your direct reports?

2	1	0
Can Act Directly Or Recommend With High Effectiveness	Can Recommend but With Mixed Results	No

3. Do you have the knowledge necessary to assign tasks to direct reports and instruct them in task completion?

2	1	0
Yes	Sometimes or In some aspects	No

4. Is it your job to evaluate the performance of your direct reports?

2	1	0
Yes	Sometimes or In some aspects	No

5. Have you been given an official title of authority by the organization (for example, manager, director, department head)?

2	0
Yes	No

Scoring

Sum responses to all items for your position power score.

Group atmosphere is a common means used by experts to characterize different management jobs' reflection of their social system characteristics. This book proposes that all managers should periodically examine their group atmosphere and consider how changes in their own work routines or in organizational policies may impact that dimension (see Table 3.2).

An excellent self-assessment form is given in the study by Fiedler et al. (1976) for measuring a group's social characteristics or group atmosphere. This eight-item rating form is easily completed by any manager in minutes and describes both leader to member relations and member to member relations.

Table 3.2 Examples of social system characteristics

Social system characteristic	Example
Group process	Members' needs or drives Tasks' interdependence Proximity and workflow Frequency of interactions Members' experience/skill levels
Intragroup Relationships	Individual's roles Individuals' status
Group Maintenance	Norms Conflict levels Relationship with leader

Group Atmosphere Rating Form

1. The people I supervise have trouble getting along with each other.

1	2	3	4	5
Strongly Agree	Agree	Neither Agree nor Disagree	Disagree	Strongly Disagree

2. My direct reports are reliable and trustworthy.

5	4	3	2	1
Strongly Agree	Agree	Neither Agree nor Disagree	Disagree	Strongly Disagree

3. There seems to be a friendly atmosphere among the people I supervise.

5	4	3	2	1
Strongly Agree	Agree	Neither Agree nor Disagree	Disagree	Strongly Disagree

4. My direct reports always cooperate with me in getting the job done.

5	4	3	2	1
Strongly Agree	Agree	Neither Agree nor Disagree	Disagree	Strongly Disagree

5. There is friction between my direct reports and me.

1	2	3	4	5
Strongly Agree	Agree	Neither Agree nor Disagree	Disagree	Strongly Disagree

6. My direct reports give me a good deal of help and support in getting the job done.

5	4	3	2	1
Strongly Agree	Agree	Neither Agree nor Disagree	Disagree	Strongly Disagree

7. The people I supervise work well together in getting the job done.

5	4	3	2	1
Strongly Agree	Agree	Neither Agree nor Disagree	Disagree	Strongly Disagree

8. I have good relations with the people I supervise.

5	4	3	2	1
Strongly Agree	Agree	Neither Agree nor Disagree	Disagree	Strongly Disagree

Scoring

Sum responses to all items for your group atmosphere score.

The Developmental Challenge Profile (DCP) was developed to fill the need for a tool for studying developmental components of manager's jobs. The scale assesses features of jobs that foster learning about managerial skills and perspectives. It is intended to assist young managers' search for new experiences that have the potential of building their knowledge, skills, and capabilities. The DCP includes 96 items used to cover 15 factors in total. Examples of those factors are included as follows (i.e., as published in McCauley et al., 1994). The underlying assumptions of the scale are that most valuable managerial learning occurs when managers are faced with challenging on-the-job learning situations and that such learning adds more than just more tenure or time on the job. These learning events provide an opportunity to learn (e.g., to try new behaviors or refrain from enacting old habits or ideas) as well as provide the motivation to learn as they illustrate the rewards for successfully meeting the challenges or the reactions upon avoiding uncomfortable situations. In short, responding to these items may help you understand which new or special projects to seek as you hope to develop greater skills.

The Developmental Challenge Profile

Managing Business Diversity   *Mean = 3.45, sd = 1.09*

1. You are responsible for numerous different products or technologies or services.

1	2	3	4	5
Not at all descriptive	Slightly descriptive	Moderately descriptive	Very descriptive	Extremely descriptive

Influencing Without Authority   *Mean = 3.05, sd = 0.77*

2. To achieve your most important goals, you must influence peers at similar levels in other units, functions, divisions, and so on.

1	2	3	4	5
Not at all descriptive	Slightly descriptive	Moderately descriptive	Very descriptive	Extremely descriptive

High Stakes   *Mean = 3.02, sd = 0.68*

3. You are being tested by top management.

1	2	3	4	5
Not at all descriptive	Slightly descriptive	Moderately descriptive	Very descriptive	Extremely descriptive

Job Overload   *Mean = 2.38, sd = 0.83*

4. The job requires you to put in long hours (60 or more hours a week).

1	2	3	4	5
Not at all descriptive	Slightly descriptive	Moderately descriptive	Very descriptive	Extremely descriptive

Developing New Directions   *Mean = 2.37, sd = 0.75*

5. You have to make major strategic changes in the business; its direction, structure, or operations.

1	2	3	4	5
Not at all descriptive	Slightly descriptive	Moderately descriptive	Very descriptive	Extremely descriptive

Difficult Boss   *Mean = 2.37, sd = 0.78*

6. Your boss is opposed to something you think is important to do.

1	2	3	4	5
Not at all descriptive	Slightly descriptive	Moderately descriptive	Very descriptive	Extremely descriptive

Adverse Business Conditions   *Mean = 2.22, sd = 0.73*

7. The business or major product line faces intensely competitive markets.

1	2	3	4	5
Not at all descriptive	Slightly descriptive	Moderately descriptive	Very descriptive	Extremely descriptive

Lack of Personal Support   *Mean = 2.19, sd = 0.81*

8. It's difficult to find a supportive person to talk to in this job.

1	2	3	4	5
Not at all descriptive	Slightly descriptive	Moderately descriptive	Very descriptive	Extremely descriptive

Inherited Problems   *Mean = 2.10, sd = 0.80*

9. You inherited at least one key direct report with serious performance problems.

1	2	3	4	5
Not at all descriptive	Slightly descriptive	Moderately descriptive	Very descriptive	Extremely descriptive

Problems with Employees   *Mean = 2.01, sd = 0.70*

10. Your direct reports are used to doing things the way they have always been done and are reluctant to change.

1	2	3	4	5
Not at all descriptive	Slightly descriptive	Moderately descriptive	Very descriptive	Extremely descriptive

Unfamiliar Responsibilities   *Mean = 1.99, sd = 0.77*

11. You have to manage something (e.g., a function, product technology, or market) with which you are unfamiliar.

1	2	3	4	5
Not at all descriptive	Slightly descriptive	Moderately descriptive	Very descriptive	Extremely descriptive

Lack of Top Management Support   *Mean = 1.93, sd 0.65*

12. Resources are tight; you have to scrounge and "beg, borrow, or steal" to get the job done.

1	2	3	4	5
Not at all descriptive	Slightly descriptive	Moderately descriptive	Very descriptive	Extremely descriptive

Proving Yourself   *Mean=1.84, sd=0.72*

13. Most of the people reporting to you are more experienced than you are.

1	2	3	4	5
Not at all descriptive	Slightly descriptive	Moderately descriptive	Very descriptive	Extremely descriptive

Handling External Pressure   *Mean = 1.56, sd = 0.62*

14. This job involves dealing with outside groups that can have a substantial impact on the business.

1	2	3	4	5
Not at all descriptive	Slightly descriptive	Moderately descriptive	Very descriptive	Extremely descriptive

Reduction Decisions   *Mean = 1.54, sd = 0.83*

15. You have to lay off a significant number of your people.

1	2	3	4	5
Not at all descriptive	Slightly descriptive	Moderately descriptive	Very descriptive	Extremely descriptive

Scoring

A score between 24 and 45 indicates an average developmental challenge. A score of 46 or higher indicates above average developmental challenge. A score of 23 or lower indicates below average developmental challenge.

Why Are Situational Differences Important in Organizations?

A classic case study of how an organization systematically benefited from planned developmental assignments is the well known case study of AT&T (Bray, Campbell, and Grant 1974; Howard and Bray 1988). This longitudinal research on managerial success found that tailoring the individual's job situation to be most favorable to their individual characteristics led to the greatest career advancement. "A favorable situation existed when a person was encouraged to develop management skills, was given challenging assignments with increased responsibility, and had a boss who served as a role model by setting an example of how a successful, achievement-oriented manager should act" (Yukl 2010). Citibank is another example of how systematic development of general management skills created new pathways to senior executive management positions (Clark and Lyness 1991). In this example, assignments involved either major strategic challenges or difficult people-relationship challenges.

Using case studies of career failure or derailment of executives, McCall, Lombardo, and Morrison (1988) researched what events sabotaged or diverted managers from apparently successful careers. In these researchers' opinion, each of these managers had strengths and weaknesses, but often the best explanations for their failures were beyond the managers' control (e.g., unfavorable economic conditions) or weak interpersonal skills, which were clearly clashing with the organization's culture and its demands. In short, knowledge or awareness of situational demands were a critical element in understanding how executives failed in these organizational contexts.

Researchers have explored how to make developmental assignments lead to positive organizational outcomes. For example, when assignments are too brief, they fail to provide enough feedback on the consequences of the developing manager's actions or decisions (Ohlott 1998). But staying in an assignment too long may lead to boredom too. The correct sequencing of assignments has been studied (McCall 2004). Learning basic knowledge and skills, in less challenging assignments should occur before moving on to bigger more challenging projects. Moving too quickly through the developmental assignments may also be counterproductive.

McCauley, Eastman, and Ohlott (1994) argue that organizations may benefit the most from assigning developmentally challenging positions to their managers if the organization allows the manager to share in the planning of the assignments and then to track how the assignments unfold. These authors believe that time for reflection on the experience and then discussions or journaling to allow for identifying what lessons have been learned is critical. Dechant (1994) believes that overall organizational outcomes are enhanced when concrete learning plans are applied. The individual manager should analyze the project for task objectives, context, and job requirements so that the person can recognize and take advantage of the learning opportunities embedded in any new assignment. Learning needs for others or even impacts on groups can be recognized too and thus add to the systemic benefits of the developmental assignments.

The DCP assessment included in the previous section is a valuable tool for sizing up one's current position for learning on-the-job opportunities. It calls into question, however, whether a manager can make changes in their work situation by themselves. This might be a good time to discuss mentoring on the job. Organizations have found value in creating formal mentoring systems wherein mentors are officially assigned to new or high-potential workers (Robbins and Judge 2017). Informal mentoring systems, on the other hand, allow either member of the mentor–mentee pair to make the choice to commit to an ongoing relationship. Pairing a less experienced mentee–manager with a more experienced mentor–senior manager might involve 10 or more identifiable functions (Allen et al. 2004; Murray 2002; Zachary 2000). Mentors might lobby to get the mentee more challenging assignments or to coach the mentee through experiences that facilitate developing managerial skills. A mentor can provide indirect assistance by introducing the mentee to influential managers within the organizational hierarchy of authority or even by shielding the mentee from possible risks to their reputation or status within the chain of command. In a similar vein, indirect assistance might include acting as sounding board for any ideas that the mentee might have that they would be reluctant to share with their current supervisor or performance evaluator, or the mentor can nominate or sponsor the mentee for new promotions or assignments. Some mentoring functions have an obvious social support quality such as counseling the mentee about their anxieties and questions of self-confidence or by sharing prior personal work experiences the mentor has had in the past. Finally, the mentor acts a role model and provides acceptance and emotional support to the mentee. For the mentor, this relationship has benefits too, including acting as a communication pipeline for potential organizational problems or early warning systems for needed changes, along with the personal satisfaction from helping the individual mentee and receiving validation from that less experienced manager in the process.

In summary, organizational resources like formal job rotational plans or mentoring assignments can help you develop your situational recognition competency but it is also true that building one's own system can be crafted. Finding a mentor, especially a mentor outside your immediate performance review process, can be very beneficial for you, your mentor, and your organization.

Where Can Competence in Recognizing Situational Differences Be Developed?

One way to develop situational recognition skills is to volunteer for new assignments that are significantly different from your current assignment. Yukl (2010) lists examples of such developmentally relevant assignments:

- Managing a new project or startup operation
- Serving as the department's representative to a cross-functional team
- Chairing a special task force planning a major organizational change
- Dealing with a serious operational problem
- Developing and conducting a training program

- Assuming new administrative responsibilities such as preparing a budget
- Serving as a liaison to another organization such as supplier or a client

You can keep a journal of workplace actions and situations that draw on your leadership skills and then by reexamining those situations for their contextual demands you can assess how much situational factors draw out or inhibit your natural responses.

If you are placed in a career ladder, research potential promotions in terms of how the work contexts will change with the promotions. Use the four scales listed in this chapter to evaluate what you know about new positions or to help you investigate areas where further information or insight would prove valuable. This is similar to the idea of "engineering your own leadership situation" (e.g., Fiedler and Chemers 1984, Chapter 9).

CHAPTER 4

Cognitive Competence

What Is Cognitive Competence?

Imagine yourself as a manager who works for a business that provides remediation services to end-user customers. Your company is in the business of providing postdisaster services that include cleanup and removal after such things as fires, floods, or broken water pipes. Your employer therefore puts a very high premium on customer service and the firm's ability to generate new business is a high priority for you as a manager.

You have an annual budget for advertising and you have to choose from various alternatives to place your ads in the media. You can, for example, place ads in newspapers and magazines, or ads on the radio, or commercials on the television, or promote your service via billboards and signs, or you can choose promotion via Internet ads, or even through such media as Angie's List, or various blogs and bulletin boards. As a manager, it is your task to take the annual budget for such public promotion of your service and produce the greatest sales revenues in the coming year. How then do you go about choosing where to place your advertising to produce the greatest revenue boost? Clearly relying simply on word-of-mouth from prior customers is not going to be sufficient to grow your company's business, so you must choose carefully and wisely in order to increase your market share as well is your net income.

How does a manager in this particular situation go about making such a decision? I think we can probably assume that the individual involved in this type of decision not only has limited funds but also has limited time in which to make the decision. It's also true that media representatives call on such managers and try and pitch their advertising as the best alternative. This all produces a situation in which all of the various claims and counterclaims have to be weighed, analyzed, and evaluated. In sum then, this makes it a good example of organizational decision making. Let us consider how can we improve our decision-making skills by understanding where we can improve and then determine what kinds of experiences on the job can help us build these skills.

How Decision Making Deviates From True Rationality

Recently, the information technology (IT) department where I work notified me that I was due for a new laptop. My organization has a policy of replacing computers every two years, and my group was due for replacements. As they manage these vendor relationships carefully, each person of my rank is offered the choice between three machines: A PC platform laptop, an OS platform laptop, and a notebook. All three are machines are outfitted by my organization's IT department so they are all capable of running our most common software packages and all cost the organization about the same amount of money. So unlike the situation when I buy my own personal computer, price is not a primary criterion.

Now since I am a professor you might guess that I sat down with a pencil and paper and formally compared each of the options on the basis of a number of important criteria. Those decision standards might include battery life factors, screen size, memory capacity, clock speed, reputed reliability, and so on. But in this case my behavior was an excellent example of biased decision making since I chose the option which had the best result on only one criterion: weight. This was biased decision making at its best: The use of a single criterion that was highly available (e.g., I had been recently complaining about carrying my old laptop to meetings) and it illustrated satisficing on all other criteria.

Biased decision making is not always going to make a manager arrive at a bad decision. In this case, I really like my new computer. However, looking at behavior over a range of decisions might be very informative and allow one to see how one's decisions vary from strict rationality. In fact, knowing your own tendencies toward bias might help you spot biases or errors in others' decision making (Hardman and Hardman 2009; Harrison 1999; Kahneman 2003; Kahneman, Slovic, and Tversky 1982). In this case, awareness is one of the best training or skill development activities possible.

How Can Cognitive Competence Be Assessed?

To help you get a sense of where your decision-making skills are, complete the following Cognitive Reflection Test (Toplak, West, and Stanovich 2011).

The Cognitive Reflection Test

Following are a number of problems for you to consider. As you will see, they represent a wide range of real-life situations. Think carefully about each problem, and then select the answers that are sensible to you.

1. The Caldwells had long ago decided that when it was time to replace their car, they would get what they called "one of those solid, safety-conscious, built-to-last Swedish cars"—either a Volvo or a Saab. As luck would have it, their old car gave up the ghost on the last day of the closeout sale for the model year both for the Volvo and for the Saab. The model year was changing for both cars and the dollar had recently dropped substantially against European currencies; therefore, if they waited to buy either a Volvo or a Saab, it would cost them substantially more—about $1,200. They quickly got out their Consumer Reports where they found that the consensus of the experts was that both cars were very sound mechanically, although the Volvo was felt to be slightly superior on some dimensions. They also found that the readers of Consumer Reports who owned a Volvo reported having somewhat fewer mechanical problems than owners of Saabs. They were about to go and strike a bargain with the Volvo dealer when Mr. Caldwell remembered that they had two friends who owned a Saab and one who owned a Volvo. Mr. Caldwell called up the friends. Both Saab owners reported having had a few mechanical problems but nothing major. The Volvo owner exploded when asked how he liked his car. "First that fancy fuel injection computer thing went out: $250 bucks. Next, I started having trouble with the rear end. Had to replace it. Then the transmission and the clutch. I finally sold it after 3 years for junk."

Given that the Caldwells are going to buy either a Volvo or a Saab today, in order to save $1,200, which do you think they should buy?

a. Buy the Volvo

b. Buy the Saab

2. A certain town is served by two hospitals. In the larger hospital about 45 babies were born each day, and in the smaller hospital about 15 babies were born each day. As you know, about 50 percent of all babies are boys. The exact percentage of baby boys, however, varies from day to day. Sometimes it is higher than 50 percent, and sometimes it is lower.

For a period of over a year, each hospital recorded the days on which more than 60 percent of the babies born were boys. Which hospital do you think recorded more such days?

a. The larger hospital

b. The smaller hospital

c. About the same (i.e., within 5 percent of each other)

3. As you know, the game of squash can be played to either 9 or 15 points. Holding all other rules of the game constant, if A is a better player than B, which scoring system will give A a better chance of winning?

a. A game to 9 points

b. A game to 15 points

c. About the same (i.e., the scoring system should make no difference)

4. After the first two weeks of the major league baseball season, newspapers begin to print the top 10 batting averages. Typically, after two weeks, the leading batter often has an average of about .450. However, no batter in major league history has ever averaged .450 at the end of the season. Why do you think this is?

a. When a batter is known to be hitting for a high average, pitchers bear down more when they pitch to him.

b. Pitchers tend to get better over the course of a season, as they get more in shape. As pitchers improve, they are more likely to strike out batters, so batters' averages do down.

c. A player's high average at the beginning of the season may be just luck. The longer season provides a more realistic test of a batter's skill.

    d. A batter who has such a hot streak at the beginning of the season is under a lot of stress to maintain his performance record. Such stress adversely affects his playing.

    e. When a batter is known to be hitting for a high average, he stops getting good pitches to hit. Instead, pitchers "play the corners" of the plate because they don't mind walking him.

5. When playing slot machines, people win something like one in every 10 times. Julie, however, has just won on her first three plays. What are her chances of winning the next time she plays?

    a. 1 out of 10 times

    b. 2 out of 10 times

    c. 3 out of 10 times

    d. 4 out of 10 times

    e. 5 out of 10 times

    f. 6 out of 10 times

    g. 7 out of 10 times

    h. 8 out of 10 times

    i. 9 out of 10 times

    j. 10 out of 10 times

6. Imagine that we are tossing a fair coin (a coin that has a 50/50 chance of coming up heads or tails) and it has just come up heads five times in a row. For the sixth toss, do you think that:

    a. It is more likely that tails will come up than heads.

    b. It is more likely that heads will come up than tails.

    c. Heads and tails are equally probable on the sixth toss.

7. Linda is 31 years old, single, outspoken, and very bright. She majored in philosophy. As a student, she was deeply concerned with issues of discrimination and social justice, and also participated in antinuclear demonstrations.

    a. Linda is a teacher in an elementary school.

    b. Linda works in a bookstore.

    c. Linda is active in the feminist movement.

    d. Linda is a psychiatric social worker.

    e. Linda is a member of the League of Women Voters.

    f. Linda is a bank teller.

    g. Linda is an insurance salesperson.

    h. Linda is a bank teller and is active in the feminist movement.

8. A doctor had been working on a cure for a mysterious disease. Finally, he created a drug that he thinks will cure people of the disease. Before he can begin to use it regularly, he has to test the drug. He selected 300 people who had the disease and gave them the drug to see what happened. He selected 100 people who had the disease and did not give them the drug in order to see what happened. The table below indicates what the outcome of the experiment was:

	Cured	Not cured
Treatment present	200	100
Treatment absent	75	25

Circle the number below that reflects your judgment of the drug's effectiveness:

-10 -9 -8 -7 -6 -5 -4 -3 -2 -1 0 +1 +2 +3 +4 +5 +6 +7 +8 +9 +10
Highly ineffective   Highly effective

9. The city of Middleopolis has had an unpopular police chief for a year and a half. He is a political appointee who is a crony of the mayor, and he had little previous experience in police administration when he was appointed. The mayor has recently defended the chief in public, announcing that in the time since he took office, crime rates decreased by 12 percent. Which of the following pieces of evidence would most deflate the mayor's claim that his chief is competent?

a. The crime rates of the two cities closest to Middleopolis in location and size have decreased by 18 percent in the same period.

b. An independent survey of the citizens of Middleopolis shows that 40 percent more crime is reported by respondents in the survey than is reported in police records.

c. Common sense indicates that there is little a police chief can do to lower crime rates. These are for the most part due to social and economic conditions beyond the control of officials.

d. The police chief has been discovered to have business contacts with people who are known to be involved in organized crime.

10. Imagine yourself meeting David Maxwell. Your task is to assess the probability that he is a university professor based on some information you will be given. This will be done in two steps. At each step, you will get some information that you may or may not find useful in making your assessment. After each piece of information, you will be asked to assess the probability that David Maxwell is a university professor. In doing so, consider all the information you have received to that point if you consider it to be relevant. Your probability assessments should be numbers between 0 and 1 that express your degree of belief—1 means that "I am absolutely certain that he is a university professor"; 0.65 means "The chances are 65 out of 100 that he is a university professor"; and so forth. You may use any number between 0 and 1, for example, 0.15, 0.95, and so on.

    Step 1: You are told that David Maxwell attended a party in which 25 male university professors and 75 male business executives took part, 100 people all together. Question: What do you think the probability is that David Maxwell is a university professor?

    Step 2: You are told that David Maxwell is a member of the Bears Club. Seventy percent of the male university professors mentioned at the abovementioned party were members of the Bears Club, and 90 percent of the business executives at the party were members of the Bears Club. Question: What do you think the probability is that David Maxwell is a university professor?

11. Problem 1: Imagine that the United States is preparing for the outbreak of unusual Asian disease, which is expected to kill 600 people. Two alternative programs to combat the disease have been proposed. Assume that the exact scientific estimates of the consequences of the programs are as follows: If Program A is adopted, 200 people will be saved. If Program B is adopted, there is a one-third probability that 600 will be saved, and a two-thirds probability that no people will be saved. Which of the two programs do you favor?

    a. Program A

    b. Program B

    Problem 2: If Program C is adopted, 400 people will be saved. If Program D is adopted, there is a one-third probability that no will die and a two-thirds probability that 600 people will die. Which of the two programs do you favor?

a. Program C

b. Program D

12. Assume that you are presented with two trays of black and white marbles: a large tray that contains 100 marbles and a small tray that contains 10 marbles. The marbles are spread in a single layer on each tray. You must draw out one marble (without peeking, of course) from either tray. If you draw a black marble, you win $2. Consider a condition is which the small tray contains 1 black marble and 9 white marbles, and the large tray contains 8 black marbles and 92 white marbles. From which tray would you prefer to select a marble in a real situation?

a. The small tray

b. The large tray

13. A die with four red faces and two green faces will be rolled 60 times. Before each roll, you will be asked to predict which color (red or green) will show up once the die is rolled. You will be given one dollar for each correct prediction. Assume that you want to make as much money as possible. What strategy would you use in order to make *as much money as possible* by making the most correct predictions?

Strategy A: Go by intuition, switching when there has been too many of one color or the other.

Strategy B: Predict the more likely color (red) on most of the rolls, but occasionally, after a long run of reds, predict a green.

Strategy C: Make predictions according to the frequency of occurrence (four of six for red and two of six for green). That is, predict twice as many reds as greens.

Strategy D: Predict the more likely color (red) on all of the 60 rolls.

Strategy E: Predict more red than green, but switching back and forth depending upon "runs" of one color or the other.

14. Imagine that you are staying in a hotel room and that you have just paid $6.95 to see a movie on pay TV. Assume that five minutes into the movie you are bored with the movie and that the movie seems pretty bad. Do you

a. continue to watch the movie?

b. switch to a different channel?

Next, imagine that you start watching a second movie and that five minutes into that movie you are bored, and the movie seems pretty bad. Do you

a. continue to watch the movie?

b. switch to a different channel?

15. Case 1: A 55-year-old man had a heart condition. He had to stop working because of chest pain. He enjoyed his work and did not want to stop. His pain also interfered with other things, such as travel and recreation. A type of bypass operation would relieve his pain and increase his life expectancy from age 65 to 70. However, 8 percent of the people who have this operation die from the operation itself.

His physician decided to go ahead with the operation. The operation succeeded. Evaluate the physician's decision to go ahead with the operation. Circle your answer:

1	2	3	4	5	6	7
Incorrect						Correct
A bad						An excellent
decision						decision

Case 2: A 55-year-old man had a bad hip. He had to stop working because of the hip pain. He enjoyed his work and did not want to stop. His pain also interfered with other things, such as travel and recreation. A type of hip replacement operation would relieve his pain and increase his life expectancy from age 65 to 70. However, 2 percent of the people who have this operation die from the operation itself. His physician decided to go ahead with the operation. The operation failed and the patient died. Evaluate the physician's decision to go ahead with the operation. Circle your answer:

1	2	3	4	5	6	7
Incorrect						Correct
A bad decision						An excellent decision

Scoring

Answer Explanations

1. *Choosing b is evidence of the causal base rate bias. Choosing a is the unbiased choice.*

2. *Choosing a or c is evidence for the insensitivity to sample size bias. b is the unbiased choice.*

3. *Choosing a or c is evidence for the insensitivity to sample size bias. b is the unbiased choice.*

4. *Choosing any answer other than c is evidence for the regression to the mean bias.*

5. *Choosing any answer other than a is evidence for the gambler's fallacy bias.*

6. *Choosing any answer other than c is evidence for the gambler's fallacy bias.*

7. *Choosing h is evidence for the conjunction bias. All other choices are nonbiased.*

8. *Choosing any response from 0 to +10 is evidence for failing to detect covariation. Choosing any negative number is showing correct covariance detection.*

9. *Choosing any alternative other than a is failing to show methodological reasoning.*

10. *Any adjustment in step 2 that lowers the probability from step 1 shows correct Bayesian reasoning. Any other adjustment raising the probability shows bias.*

11. *Choosing a for both problems or choosing b for both problems avoids the framing bias. Choosing either a and then b or b and then a is evidence for the framing bias.*

12. *Choosing a shows correct probabilistic reasoning.*

13. *Choosing strategy D shows correct probability matching.*

14. *Choosing a for both problems or choosing b for both problems avoids the sunk cost bias. Choosing either a and then b or b and then a is evidence for the sunk cost bias.*

15. *If the rating for case 1 is equal to or lower than the rating for case 2 the answer is correct. If the rating for case 1 is higher than the rating for case 2 is shows evidence of outcome bias.*

Overall Test Scoring

A correct answer for each problem receives a score of 1 and an incorrect answer receives a score of 0. Summing the scores produces a range of scores from 0 to 15. The mean score is 6.88 and the standard deviation is 2.32. This means that if your score is 9 or more your score is in the top 20 percent and you are above average in your decision-making skills. If your score is 5 or less, your score is in the bottom 20 percent and you are very prone to decision-making errors.

Why Is Cognitive Competence Important in Organizations?

True rationality and bounded rationality are different. In many managerial contexts, a primary goal of decision making is rationality (LeBoeuf 2002; March and Simon 1958) because this way of making decisions emphasizes the quality of the manager's judgments as well as the quality of the manager's final choice. In other words, the manager makes consistent value maximizing choices within prespecified constraints on their decision making. One way of describing this rational decision making is to refer to it as a seven-step decision-making process (see Figure 4.1). Let's take a moment and look at the seven-step process, which has been called econologic or true rationality.

The first step is described as recognizing that a problem exists. A problem exists when there is a discrepancy that exists between the desired state and what is currently observed in the operating environment. If you calculate current operating expenses and check that you have spent significantly more than your department or unit's budget, then you have some idea that a problem exists. Once a problem solver or decision maker has identified a problem, that manager needs to identify the decision criteria that will be important in solving the problem (i.e., step 2). In other words, criteria that will help the decision maker to determine what relevant standards to apply in making the decision. Thus, the manager's interests, values, and preferences can enter into the decision-making process. Identifying the organization's criteria which are important is necessary as well as the organization's goals that must be satisfied in making the

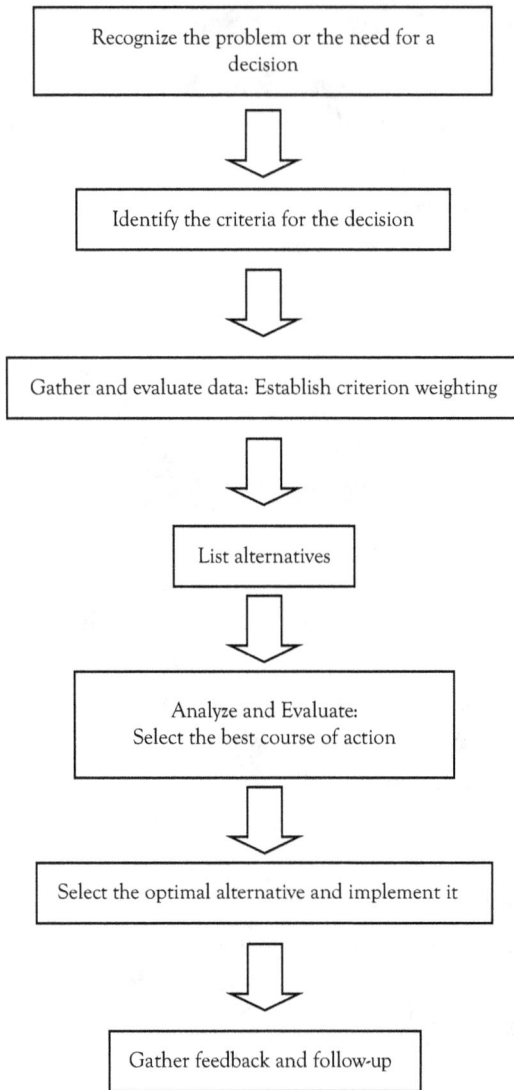

Figure 4.1 The steps of pure rationality in decision making

decision. Keep in mind that factors that might determine the final judgment that are not included in the criteria then become irrelevant to the
final decision, so specifying them at this point is crucial to ensuring decision quality in the end. Thus, this is quite a critical step as it influences
both the judgments to be made and the final choice activity.

The third step might be described as weighting the previously identified criteria in importance to help create priorities relevant to the decision.

It is relatively rare in organizational life when all the criteria are equal in importance. Equal weights might work in academic or teaching examples, but they rarely represent the type of organizational reality managers face. Simplifying examples might make textbooks easier to read, but the relative weighting of criteria is one of the hallmarks of expert, not novice, managerial decision making. For instance, at times cost savings is the highest priority while at another time scheduling or delivery to the customer may take a far higher priority.

The fourth step requires the decision maker generate possible alternatives from which to choose a final solution. This step is intended to be merely the identification of the alternatives and does not necessarily imply that you are systematic in listing these possibilities. Comparison or evaluation activity will begin in the next step. Once the alternatives have been generated, the decision maker can begin the difficult analysis and evaluation of each alternative (i.e., step 5). Systematically comparing each alternative on each criterion allows the decision maker to calculate strengths and weaknesses for each alternative. The sixth step requires selecting the optimal alternative. This is done by evaluating each alternative against the weighted criteria in order to calculate which alternative leads the organization to the highest benefit. The final step involves gathering feedback on the optimal alternative as implemented and following up on continuing hindrances to success.

There are at least six assumptions behind the rational model (Simon 1979, 1986). This model is based on economics and logic, so we should be explicit in thinking about these assumptions and so let us list them out here. The first assumption is called problem clarity. This assumption requires that all managerial problems be clear and unambiguous and that the decision maker have complete information regarding the decision situation. Clearly, in many organizational contexts this is not a valid assumption because in fact often key information is unavailable or even unknowable. If we reflect on our example of the remediation manager, this decision maker can't know when floods or fires are going to happen even if that might make his or her task easier. A second assumption holds that the decision maker can identify all relevant criteria and can list all the relevant viable alternatives. This means that the decision maker is aware of all of the possible consequences of each alternative. In decision theory, scholars sometimes talk about decision making in terms of risk, meaning that outcomes and values are known to be variable or at least probable. Simply put, managers have to deal in probabilities. Experts in decision theory also talk about decision making under uncertainty, meaning that when outcomes or values are completely uncertain or unknown. In both cases, risk and uncertainty happen very frequently in business life. If our manager buys ads on a music service like Pandora, it is hard to know with certainty what demographic segments will hear that ad.

A third assumption is clear preferences. The rational model assumes that the criteria for all alternatives can be ranked and weighted to reflect their importance. The idea that clear preferences produce easily agreed upon weights for the relevant criteria is oftentimes violated. People are imperfect calculators and organizations often have fuzzy values that can be applied only in a vague sense. For instance, our remediation service may weigh square footage equally regardless of whether it is in stand-alone house, an apartment building, or business within a high-rise build-ing. Service in an apartment building might have reduced costs the others don't have, and the square footage pricing may fail to reflect that fact. A fourth assumption is that preferences for specific criteria are constant and that the weights assigned to them are stable over time. This too cre-ates fuzziness in the decision-making process. Managers in most indus-tries will argue that change is actually what is constant. Additionally, this assumption presupposes that there are no time or cost constraints that might limit the decision maker (e.g., the failure of essential equipment may reduce the value of signing up new clients). Thus, the truly ratio-nal decision maker should obtain full information about the alternatives and the criteria on which to choose among the alternatives because it's assumed that there are no time or cost constraints. For example, managers rarely have enough time to do a complete proactive search that produces useful information for every decision they make, even for very import-ant decisions. Time is valuable and information is oftentimes incomplete. Again, in our example a manager may not investigate every media form for its suitability for the manager's ads.

The final assumption might seem like one that would be easily met. The rational decision maker should choose among the alternatives to find a solution that yields the highest perceived value for the firm. This is seeking the maximum return for the firm's time and money. Maximum payoff in terms of dollars and cents is clearly related to business values, but the fact is that frequently decisions are made on more emotional or perhaps attitudinal grounds. We don't always choose that alternative that produces the greatest utility. The pressures of business life lead many of us as decision makers to be happy with a satisfactory outcome, even when we suspect it might not be the optimum or very best alternative. Our example manager may choose the Pandora ads mainly because the manager listens to that service and likes to hear the ads as they are broadcast. It may in fact not be the best-weighted alternative.

About 50 years ago, Simon (1972) produced a groundbreaking academic work in decision theory, which came to be known as bounded rationality. In bounded rationality Simon described not a normative system for making judgments but rather a descriptive system for making judgments. A descriptive system describes how managers actually behave in organizational contexts, whereas a normative system describes how they should function if they are perfectly rational. For example, we can look at several ways of delineating what rational behavior dictates in the normative sense and compare that to what we think managers actually do in a descriptive sense (see Table 4.1).

Cognitive Biases Managers Should Avoid

Probably the most obvious indication of bounded rationality in managerial thinking is satisficing or settling for the first acceptable alternative, thereby ending any further cognitive work to seek an optimum solution. But unfortunately, there are many more and some of these are common in organizational life. In the following paragraphs, we will describe some of these biases and then attempt to indicate how common each may be. Each of the following are heuristics, which are simple rules governing judgment or decision making or "judgmental shortcuts that generally get us where we need to go—and quickly—but at the cost of occasionally sending us off course" (Tversky and Kahneman 1974). Heuristics are a common and nearly universal cognitive aid because they lead to effort reduction and simplification in decision making (Shah and Oppenheimer 2008).

Table 4.1 Assumptions of the rational decision process and descriptive behavior of practicing managers

Rational model assumptions	Decision process behavior ideal illustrating rationality	Actual managerial behavior illustrating bounded rationality
Problem clarity	The problem is clear and unambiguous The decision maker possesses complete information relevant to the problem	Managers reduce problem contexts to simplify processing and consider only the most important parties to the decision
Known options	All viable alternatives can be listed and all possible consequences of each alternative are known	Alternatives are recalled from past problem-solving attempts or alternatives that are easily understood are used
Clear preferences	All alternatives decision criteria can be ranked and weighted by importance	Data that are available and feasible for weighted are relied on
Constant preferences	Weights for decision criteria are stable over time	Change concerning alternatives, criteria, and weights occurs frequently
Data quality	Decision maker obtains full information about both alternatives and criteria	Incomplete data are ignored or replaced by estimates
Maximum payoffs	Choose the alternative that yields the highest perceived value	Alternatives are considered sequentially and the first acceptable alternative is chosen (satisficing not optimizing)

A good first example of a cognitive bias or heuristic is the *availability* heuristic. This heuristic is a mental shortcut that relies on easily recalled examples that come to a given person's mind when evaluating a specific topic, concept, method, or decision. Availability illustrates the principle that if something can be recalled from memory, it must be important, or at least more important than exemplars, which are not as readily recalled. It is as if we say to ourselves, "If I can think of it, it must be important." Through its use, people come to weigh heavily more recent information toward their judgments, which means that new opinions are biased toward that latest news learned. When considering potential courses of action, it is true that more important consequences tend to be linked to easily available ideas. So, for example, "If only I had taken the shorter way home from work I would not have been in that auto accident yesterday" is an excellent example of a highly available counterfactual to the actual series of events. In other words, the easier it is to recall the consequences of something the greater those consequences are linked to alternative courses of action that lead to better outcomes.

Anchoring and adjustment is a bias that occurs when an individual relies too heavily on an initial piece of information offered (considered to be the "anchor") when making decisions. Anchoring occurs when a person relies on an initial piece of information to make subsequent judgments and fails to adjust that anchor when other or new data suggest it should be revised. Those objects near the anchor tend to be assimilated toward it and those further away tend to be displaced in the other direction (i.e., seen as even more extreme and irrelevant). Tversky and Kahneman (1974) asked research participants to estimate the final product for two separate calculations:

$$9 \times 7 \times 6 \times 5 \times 4 \times 3 \times 2 \times 1$$

versus

$$1 \times 2 \times 3 \times 4 \times 5 \times 6 \times 7 \times 8$$

Participants, prior to making any of the calculations, estimated the answer for the first calculation to be 2,250, but for the second they estimated the answer to be 512 (i.e., there were two different groups of participants, so none saw both calculations). This simple example shows how powerful the anchoring effect can be. Once the value of this anchor is set, all future estimates are thought of in relation to the anchor. For example, the initial price offered for a used car, set either before or at the start of negotiations, sets an arbitrary focal point for all following discussions. Prices discussed in negotiations that are lower than the anchor may seem reasonable, perhaps even cheap to the buyer, even if said prices are still relatively higher than the actual market value of the car.

Tversky and Kahneman defined *representativeness* as "the degree to which [an event] (1) is similar in essential characteristics to its parent population, and (2) reflects the salient features of the process by which it is generated" (Kahneman and Tversky 1972; Tversky and Kahneman 1983). When people rely on representativeness to make judgments, they are likely to judge wrongly because the fact that something is more representative does not actually make it more likely. The representative-ness heuristic when a person, in similarity of objects and organizing them based around the category prototype (e.g., like goes with like, and causes and effects should resemble each other), leaps to assume the current person/object/situation is in fact stereotypical of a category. This heuristic is used because similarity judgments are relatively easy mental computations. The problem is that people overestimate its ability to accurately predict the likelihood of an event. Thus, it can result in the neglect of relevant base rates or other quantitative data. This same bias can lead decision makers to overestimate the likelihood of very rare properties and to underestimate the likelihood of very common attributes. Independence of probabilistic events is a cognitive bias when ignored and this is related to the representativeness heuristic. The so-called gambler's fallacy of belief that after a long series of heads, the next coin flip must surely be a tails result, when in fact each flip is an independent but probabilistic outcome (see Figure 4.2 for another example). Tversky and Kahneman (1971) thought this implied a belief in inanimate objects' abilities such that they acted with "a memory and moral sense." In other nonprobabilistic domains, representativeness may lead to causes similar in nature to effects to be linked while dissimilar causes are systematically slighted. As an example, complex plots to assassinate the president are linked to an unexpected presidential murder much more easily than the wild aspirations of lone gunman (e.g., the Central Intelligence Agency [CIA] plots and Kennedy being linked more easily than Oswald and Kennedy).

Many fans of basketball believe that players sometimes demonstrate a 'hot hand' or a hot streak such that the shooter's odds of sinking a shot go up when they have already hit one or more shots in consecutively. Three cognitive psychologists examined the statistical records for the 1980-1981 Philadelphia 76er's star player Julius Erving, also known as Dr. J. The table below shows that the evidence doesn't support the idea even for the very best players at the peak of their career.

Overall Shooting Percentage for Shooting	Percentage of Shots Made After Sinking the First Shot	Percentage of Shots Made After Sinking Two Shots	Percentage of Shots Made After Sinking Three Shots
52%	53%	52%	48%

Figure 4.2 The myth of the hot hand

Confirmation bias is the tendency to search for or favor information in a way that confirms one's preexisting beliefs or hypotheses (Plous 1993). Since this bias affects the individual's tendencies to notice or perceive and it biases inductive reasoning, it can be considered a cognitive heuristic (Wason 1968). This bias in gathering data or remembering information selectively, or when they interpret data in a biased way becomes even stronger for desired outcomes, emotionally charged issues, and for deeply held beliefs. This also occurs when people interpret ambiguous evidence as supporting their existing position. Biased search, interpretation, and memory have been invoked to explain polarization of attitudes (e.g., when a disagreement becomes more extreme even though the different parties are exposed to the same evidence), the persistence of beliefs (e.g., when beliefs persist after the evidence for them is shown to be false), the irrational primacy effect (e.g., a greater reliance on information encountered early in a series), and *illusory correlation* (e.g., when people falsely perceive an association between two events or situations).

Escalation of commitment is a human behavior pattern in which an individual or group facing increasingly negative outcomes from a decision, action, or investment nevertheless continues the behavior instead of altering course. The decision maker continues behaviors that are irrational but align with previous decisions and actions (Staw 1997). Economists and behavioral scientists use a related term, *sunk cost fallacy*, to describe the justification of increased investment of money and/or time in a decision, based on the cumulative prior investment (i.e., the "sunk cost") despite new evidence suggesting that the cost, beginning immediately, of continuing the decision outweighs the expected benefit.

Framing relates to the decision maker's orientation toward risk. Risk aversion influences decision making to the extent that individuals are averse to risk when it is related to maintaining favorable or desirable outcomes but then are risk tolerant in order to avoid adverse or undesired outcomes (see Figure 4.3). Tversky and Kahneman (1981) used the following scenario: "Drug A will save 200 of 600 patients but Drug B will have a one-in-three chance all 600 will be saved but a two-in-three chance all 600 will die." Such a framing of the data produces risk aversion as Drug A is more likely to be chosen than Drug B. However, when the same numbers are phrased differently: "Drug A will lead to 400 of 600 patients dying but Drug B if used will have a one-in-three chance that no one will die but a two-in-three chance that everyone will die," research participants were more likely to choose Drug B. Since the logic and the numbers are identical in each scenario statement, it is their framing that produces either tolerance for risk or aversion to risk.

Hindsight bias, sometimes known as the knew-it-all-along phenomenon or creeping determinism, refers to the common tendency for people to perceive events that have already occurred as having been more predictable than they were before the events took place (Fischhoff 1975; Fischhoff, Slovic, and Lichtenstein 1977; Lichtenstein and Fischhoff 1977). As a result, people often believe after an event has occurred that they would have predicted what the outcome of the event would have been before the event occurred. Hindsight bias may cause distortions of our memories of what we knew and/or believed before an event occurred, and it

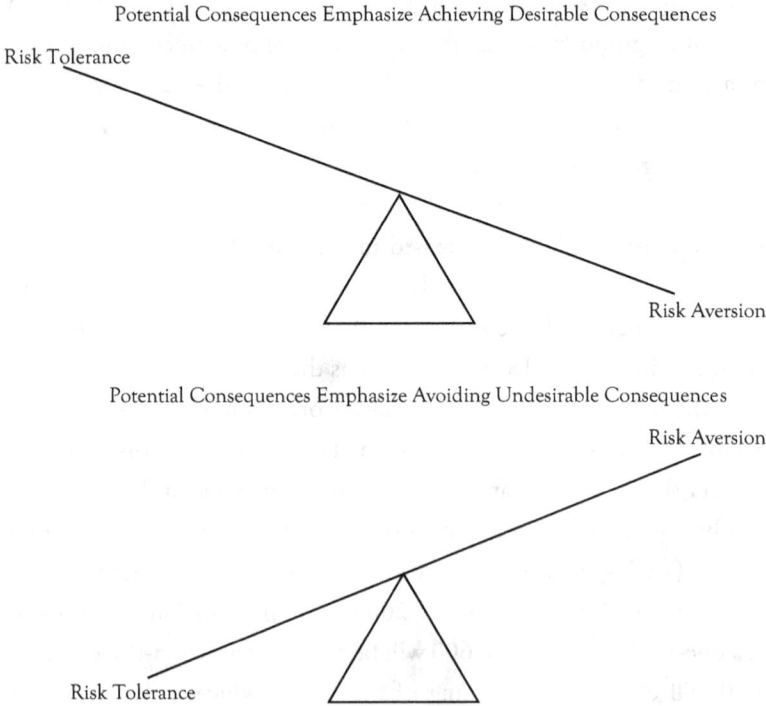

Figure 4.3 Decision framing and risk

is a significant source of overconfidence regarding our ability to predict the outcomes of future events. Fischoff (1975) gave research participants some general knowledge questions, asking each person to select an answer to each question. He then asked individuals to estimate the probability that they answered the question correctly. A second group of participants saw the same questions but were then given the correct answer. This second group was asked to estimate how likely they would have selected the correct answer in a demand situation. Participants gave much higher probabilities in the second group, demonstrating hindsight bias.

Projection is an ego defense in which the individual's ego defends itself against unconscious impulses or qualities (both positive and negative) by denying their existence within the individual's own self-concept, but then in turn attributing those same qualities to others (Freud 1996). For example, a person who is habitually overly critical of others may constantly accuse other people of being overly critical. It incorporates both biases in perception and in reasoning and therefore is a cognitive bias.

A *contrast* effect is the enhancement or diminishment, relative to normal, of a fact or statement or relevant performance as a result of successive (immediately previous) or simultaneous exposure to a stimulus of lesser or greater value in the same dimension. In this case, normal perception or cognition or performance is that which would be obtained in the absence of the comparison stimulus, that is, one based on all previous experience. A basic perceptual example: A neutral gray target will appear lighter or darker than it does in isolation when immediately preceded by, or simultaneously compared to, respectively, a dark gray or light gray target. A basic cognitive example: A person will appear more attractive than that person does in isolation when immediately preceded by, or simultaneously compared to, respectively, a less attractive person.

The *recency* effect holds that items in a series coming last are recalled and given more weight than items coming earlier in the series. These models postulate that later list items are retrieved from a highly accessible short-term memory buffer. This allows items that are recently studied to have an advantage over those that were studied earlier, as earlier study items are retrieved with greater effort from one's long-term memory buffer.

A *self-serving bias* is any cognitive or perceptual process that is distorted by the need to maintain and enhance the perceiver's self-esteem, resulting in a tendency to perceive oneself in an overly favorable manner. It is the belief that individuals tend to attribute success to their own abilities and efforts, but attribute failure to external factors as the task, the situation, or co-workers (Pal 2007). When individuals reject the validity of negative feedback, focus on their strengths and achievements but overlook their faults and failures, or take more responsibility for their group's work than they give to other members, they are protecting their ego from threat and injury. These cognitive and perceptual tendencies perpetuate illusions and error, but they also serve the self's need for esteem. For example, a student who attributes earning a good grade on an exam to their own intelligence and preparation but attributes earning a poor exam grade to the teacher's poor teaching ability or unfair test questions might be exhibiting the self-serving bias. Studies have shown that similar attributions are made in various situations, such as the workplace.

The *base rate fallacy*, also called base rate neglect or base rate bias, is a cognitive bias (Fallacy Files 2019). If presented with base rate information (i.e., potentially relevant general information) and specific information (information pertaining only to a certain case), an individual tends to ignore the base rate data and focus on the latter specific case relevant information. On the surface it might seem that when you have both generic and specific information, it might seem reasonable to ignore the general information in favor of the more specific. This would indeed be the right thing to do if you have only one type of information, but you should use all information you have. This is an application of a principle of inductive logic called "the requirement of total evidence," which requires that all relevant evidence be used in inductive reasoning. This has been found to be true in dealing with probabilities when in a decision-making role.

Independence of events is commonly ignored as important in judging the frequency of a specific event. This bias, sometimes referred to as the gambler's fallacy, fails to treat each event occurrence as separate or independent. Figure 4.2 shows a graphic example of the gambler's fallacy and is captioned as "the myth of the hot hand."

In probability theory and inferential statistics, the *law of large numbers* is a theorem that describes the result of performing the same experiment a large number of times. According to the law, the mean of the results obtained from a large number of trials should be close to the expected value or population mean; thus estimates based on more data tend to more accurate (*Encyclopedia of Mathematics* 2010). This is related to the principle of regression to the mean and is frequently seen when individuals use extreme results to predict new outcomes when less extreme results are more likely mathematically. See Table 4.2 for a summary of these biases and Table 4.3 for an estimate of their frequency of occurrence.

Where Can Cognitive Competence Be Developed?

Early attempts at de-biasing decision making were not very successful. Fischhoff (1982) reviewed four ways that experts had examined at de-biasing: (1) offering warnings about how biases might occur, (2) describing to individuals how biases might affect the direction their decisions might take, (3) providing individuals with feedback on their decision making illustrating their biases, and (4) training individuals with personalized feedback on their own decision making to illustrate their personal use of biases. Only the fourth method showed any impact, leading Fischhoff to conclude that conscious efforts or intentions to do better in the future were not enough. A possible explanation for this is the tendency for cognitive processes to become automatic, implicit, and intuitive over time (Kahneman 2011; Stanovich and West 2000). This is contrasted with cognition, which is conscious, effortful, explicit, and logical. The automatic processes are called System 1 thinking and the conscious processes are called System 2 thinking. Consequently, to develop greater cognitive competency one needs to move more cognition from System 1 back into System 2 type thinking.

Suggestions for successful de-biasing (Milkman, Chugh, and Brazerman 2009; Shang and Highhouse 2018) would therefore include individuals: (1) replacing intuitive decision making with the use of formal, analytical, and linear processes similar to simple formulas for weighting data and then combining data sources, (2) using an outsider's perspective either by role-playing that role or by actually inviting a noninvolved but informed individual to review decision processes, and (3) considering multiple options simultaneously rather than by considering each decision option

Table 4.2 Biases leading away from purely rational decision making

Biases and errors	Manager acts with bounded rationality	Manager acts with pure rationality
Availability	Judging likelihood of a disaster based on memory of media coverage	Judging likelihood of a disaster based on National Oceanic and Atmospheric Administration (NOAA) statistical evidence
Anchoring and adjustment	Relying on initial estimate of square footage by owner that is greatly inflated	Revising the estimate of square footage provided by owner with later precise measures
Representativeness	Judging employee task performance by evaluating their appearance based on cultural stereotypes	Judging employee task performance by evaluating their task-relevant actions
Confirmation	Recalling equipment failures more often about initially unfavored brands than other brands of equipment	Recalling equipment failures about initially unfavored brands as accurately as other brands of equipment
Escalation of commitment	Pursuing more, new B2B clients even after evidence of those clients not paying funds owed in a timely way	Reducing sales calls for more, new client types based on evidence of those types of clients not paying funds owed in a timely way
Framing	Describing the business as successful because of recently reduced costs	Describing recently reduced costs as balanced by increased employee turnover rates
Hindsight	Overestimating the ability to judge job applicants' later job performance by only recalling past hiring successes	Estimating the judgment of job applicants' later performance by recalling past hiring failures as well as successes
Projection	Assuming employees know as much about equipment repair as you (the manager) do	Providing detailed instructions for equipment repair to all employees until they demonstrated advanced skills
Contrast	Claiming all team members are tardy when only one team member has been late to work frequently in the recent past	All team members are evaluated on whether their own records show any tardiness in the recent past
Recency	Evaluating an employee's job performance in the most recent month more heavily than their work in the preceding 11 months	Evaluating an employee's job performance based on evidence from the entire 12 months prior to evaluation

Table 4.2 Continued

Biases and errors	Manager acts with bounded rationality	Manager acts with pure rationality
Self-serving bias	Manager attributes team success to their own contributions but attributes team failure to employees' actions	Manager does not claim success and deny their own failures but judges themselves and others on the same grounds
Base rate fallacy	Manager fails to use general information on employee lateness and focuses only on specific employee's recent late arrivals	Manager bases his reaction to an employee's recent late arrivals on fact that in general all his employees are frequently late in arriving
Independence	Believes that an industrial accident is more likely on Day 99 than on Day 9 after a previous accident	Believes workdays are separate, independent events in a chain of possible outcomes, not affected by a run of good luck
Ignoring the law of large numbers	Using the most recent month's sales revenue to predict next year's total sales	Uses a five-year moving average to predict next year's total sales

Table 4.3 Estimated percentage of correct or nonbiased responses for selected biases

Bias	Percent of correct responses (%)
Availability	53.8
Anchoring and adjustment	22.3–36.1
Representativeness	19.1
Confirmation	72.0
Escalation of commitment	64.2
Framing	62.7
Independence	23.5–92.2
Ignoring the law of large numbers	15.6–40.2

Note: Author created and adapted from Toplak, West, & Stanovich (2011). Based on sample of 346 research participants.

separately and completely before moving to the next option. Organizational level solutions to avoiding overreliance on heuristic-based decisions might include: (1) using groups, not individual decision makers whenever possible, (2) instituting training programs to develop individuals' use of statistical data in their managerial context, and (3) changing any default options within the organization to make the standard processes more explicit. Of course, a final recommendation would be to read *Thinking, Fast and Slow* by Danny Kahneman, a very enjoyable and thorough presentation of how individuals use both System 1 and System 2 cognitive processes. Finally, you can try tracking your department's or unit's decision making over a three-month period and note where and how heuristics are applied by the group or by other individuals in the group. When possible, track how avoidance of the heuristic would have altered the consequences of decisions.

CHAPTER 5

Virtual Competence

What Is Virtual Competence?

Virtual work is indicated by performance on assignments away from a traditional office or workspace using electronic technologies or when workers are free to choose to allocate their work time between multiple distant locations, in addition to spending a portion of their work week in the traditional workspace (Golden and Veiga 2008). This work arrangement has become more common in the United States and worldwide, especially since the outbreak of the COVID-19 pandemic in early 2020. While virtual work may have begun in clerical or telephone-tied occupational roles, it is common now among many professions as indicated by the growing number of major corporations permitting most of their employees the option of continuing to work at least a part of the work week virtually (Brynjolfsson, Horton, Ozimek, Rock, Sharma, and TuYe 2020). Some virtual workers work in their homes and connect to their employer's workplace electronically, whereas some virtual workers might be traveling on business to see or work with clients and therefore must connect with co-workers in their employer's workplace virtually. However, an increasingly common form of virtual work involves working with others in the same organization who might be assigned to a virtual team or special project; in this case, each team member may have a distant office or workplace (McShane and Von Glinow 2013). For example, a virtual team might include managerial budget analysts from a firm's North American office, analysts from the firm's European office, and analysts from the firm's Asian office.

Estimates of the number virtual workers vary from one survey to another, but clearly the estimates of the number of American employees working from home at least one day a month are increasing. WorldatWork (2009) estimated that in the year 2004 7.6 million U.S.-based employees worked from home, whereas in the year 2009 they estimated that over 17 million U.S.-based employees worked from home. This figure estimates how much work from home will increase substantially over the next few years and is obviously affected by such recent events as the COVID-19 pandemic. Virtual workers in established companies may, in fact, exceed more than two-thirds of the employees, reflecting those employees using electronic technologies to work from home as well as those off-site co-workers connecting with distant colleagues every week. More than 80 percent professional services and accounting firms, employing some 45,000 American employees, currently have employees who work remotely for at least 20 percent of the work week (Benko and Anderson 2010).

Virtual teams are becoming more common too (Martins, Gilson, and Maynard 2004). Groups functioning virtually are now possible because available information technology, hardware, and broadband capability allow for it (Hertel et al. 2005). Additionally, more workers are engaged in knowledge work and less are engaged in actual production work, globalization has increased the need for virtual teams, and organizations are demanding more and faster collaboration. In short, virtual teams are popular in business today and are believed to be a means to make organizations more agile and more adept at leveraging their human capital. Self-directed work teams are a related concept (Ulrich and Weber 1996), occurring whenever groups are responsible for an entire work process with a high degree of interdependence between the team members and a lack of a formal role for authority or supervision.

How Can Virtual Competence Be Assessed?

Most discussions of employees' resistance to change focus on their perceptions of how proposed changes impact the employee's self-interests on the job. But some employees resist changes that are clearly in their best interests, suggesting that these individuals resist changes in general, possibly because of their internal attributes or attitudes. The Resistance to Change Scale (Oreg 2003) is a four-factor assessment of an individual's tendencies to resist or avoid making changes across diverse organizational settings, thus indicating their degree of personal disposition toward devaluing changes generally.

Resistance to Change Scale

1. I generally consider changes to be a negative thing.

Strongly Disagree	Disagree	Slightly Disagree	Slightly Agree	Agree	Strongly Agree
1	2	3	4	5	6

2. I'll take a routine day after a day full of unexpected events any time.

Strongly Disagree	Disagree	Slightly Disagree	Slightly Agree	Agree	Strongly Agree
1	2	3	4	5	6

3. I like to do the same old things rather than trying new and different ones.

Strongly Disagree	Disagree	Slightly Disagree	Slightly Agree	Agree	Strongly Agree
1	2	3	4	5	6

4. Whenever my life forms a stable routine, I look for ways to change it.

Strongly Disagree	Disagree	Slightly Disagree	Slightly Agree	Agree	Strongly Agree
6	5	4	3	2	1

5. I'd rather be bored than surprised.

Strongly Disagree	Disagree	Slightly Disagree	Slightly Agree	Agree	Strongly Agree
1	2	3	4	5	6

6. If I were to be informed that there's going to be a significant change regarding the way things are done at work, I would probably feel stressed.

Strongly Disagree	Disagree	Slightly Disagree	Slightly Agree	Agree	Strongly Agree
1	2	3	4	5	6

7. When I am informed of a change of plans, I tense up a bit.

Strongly Disagree	Disagree	Slightly Disagree	Slightly Agree	Agree	Strongly Agree
1	2	3	4	5	6

8. When things don't go according to plans, it stresses me out.

Strongly Disagree	Disagree	Slightly Disagree	Slightly Agree	Agree	Strongly Agree
1	2	3	4	5	6

9. If my boss changed the criteria for evaluating employees, it would probably make me feel uncomfortable even if I thought I'd do just as well without having to do any extra work.

Strongly Disagree	Disagree	Slightly Disagree	Slightly Agree	Agree	Strongly Agree
1	2	3	4	5	6

10. Changing plans seems like a real hassle to me.

Strongly Disagree	Disagree	Slightly Disagree	Slightly Agree	Agree	Strongly Agree
1	2	3	4	5	6

11. Often, I feel a bit uncomfortable even about changes that may potentially improve my life.

Strongly Disagree	Disagree	Slightly Disagree	Slightly Agree	Agree	Strongly Agree
1	2	3	4	5	6

12. When someone pressures me to change something, I tend to resist it even if I think the change may ultimately benefit me.

Strongly Disagree	Disagree	Slightly Disagree	Slightly Agree	Agree	Strongly Agree
1	2	3	4	5	6

13. I sometimes fed myself avoiding changes that I know will be good for me.

Strongly Disagree	Disagree	Slightly Disagree	Slightly Agree	Agree	Strongly Agree
1	2	3	4	5	6

Scoring

Sum responses for items 1 to 5. This is your Routine Seeking score.

Low = 5 to 11   Average = 12 to 18   High = 19 to 30

Sum response for items 6 to 9. This is your Emotional Reaction score.

Low = 4 to 10   Average = 11 to 18   High = 19 to 24

Sum response for items 10 to 13. This is your Short-Term Focus score.

Low = 4 to 8   Average = 9 to 16   High = 17 to 24

Score Interpretation

Routine Seeking. Higher scores indicate a preference for low levels of stimulation and novelty.

Emotional Reactions to Imposed Changes. High scores on this factor mean that the individual feels that change implies a loss of control in their job and a belief that they will not be able to cope effectively with the stresses introduced by changes.

Short-Term Focus. High scores on this factor reflect that individuals may prefer not to enter into an adjustment period due to changes made and to report feeling uncomfortable with changes because they bring a more short-term focus to their work efforts.

A person with a very low total score on the Resistance to Change Scale would most benefit from formal training programs in which strategies for coping with the upcoming change are presented. In other words, such individuals need direct assistance in making necessary changes.

Why Is Virtual Competence Important in Organizations?

There is evidence that working from home virtually does not impact productivity negatively, but instead it may enhance productivity by promoting work–life balance. One recent study of 25,000 IBM employees showed that employees working at home performed 50 hours of work per week to 46 hours per week for those working only at the office location. Perhaps the time lost to commuting and the ease of caring for children while working made the benefits of working at home include greater productivity. Most workers report experiencing work–life tensions when their working hours exceed 30 hours per week (Hill et al. 2010). Of course, these are self-reported figures and potentially could be confirmed by online activity, but the point here is that the time spent previously on getting to work is now potentially available to make employees more productive.

Virtual work also offers environmental benefits. Cisco Systems estimates telecommuting by employees worldwide avoids almost 50,000 metric tons of greenhouse gas emissions and saves employees $10 million in fuel costs each year. The same firm states that they save nearly $30 million each year by reducing space requirements due to more employees working from home. When an imminent blizzard shuts federal government offices in Washington, DC, 30 percent of the employees worked at home virtually, saving the government $30 million per day during the storm (Meinert 2011).

Yet despite these potential benefits, virtual employees face several potential personal challenges. Family relations may suffer rather than improve if employees lack sufficient space and resources for the home office. Some employees complain of social isolation and a reduction in promotional opportunities when working away from the office. Virtual work clearly requires people who are self-motivated and organized, to work effectively with children present, or when the presence of other technologies act as potential distractions. Speaking more directly to how virtual work affects employees, especially regarding virtual work in teams, McShane and Von Glinow (2013) report that these workers complain of a lack of communication richness, of feeling less trust from their co-workers (i.e., compared to when they are located together), more concern about the way that differences in employees' cultures/beliefs/expectations may make correctly interpreting their behavior difficult at a distance, and overall that virtual employees report perceiving less control and influence over their work than when they are colocated. VitalSmarts (2009) adds that virtual teams generate far more complaints about lack of task completion, missed deadlines, unannounced changes in the work product, and more misleading or confusing information about their tasks. This suggests that some team members are poorly adjusted to virtual work. Those who are best suited to virtual work have sufficient fulfillment of social needs elsewhere in their lives. "They can be the kind of people who stayed late and did the job in the office, people who know what they're responsible for, anytime to get it done," says Michelle Bunch, president of Luncheon and Associates, an advertising and marketing firm in Longmeadow, Massachusetts (Bednar 2010). Virtual work arrangements are also more successful in organizations when they evaluate employees and their performance outcomes rather than their face time (McCloskey and Igbaria 2003). Raghuram et al. (2001) conducted a study of 756 virtual workers in a telecommunications organization seeking to examine how structural factors and relationship factors relate to the individual's adjustment to virtual work. Their results were that such structural factors as work independence and clarity of evaluation criteria had a positive predictive relationship with virtual work adjustment. Furthermore, they found that relationship factors like interpersonal trust (e.g., virtual workers must anticipate how co-workers are reacting to them since they can no longer directly observe their co-workers' reactions) and a sense of organizational connectedness (e.g., the opposite of feeling that being out of sight means they are not being attended to or that their career plans are being negatively affected by virtual work) were positive predictors of adjustment. The researchers suggest that improving relationship factors is within the possible control of many managers of virtual workers (i.e., more so than the structural factors) and point out that holding social events or adding social time to small group meetings online can build trust and a sense of connectedness (Lipnack and Stamps 2000). They suggest that arranging for mentorship connections is another way to assist virtual workers who may feel marginalized.

A common form of virtual work would be operating within self-directed teams. These teams are cross-functional groups organized around work processes. They complete an entire piece of work requiring several interdependent tasks and that have substantial discretion over the execution of those tasks. This definition includes three distinct features of self-directed work teams. First, these teams complete an entire piece of work requiring several interdependent tasks. This type of work arrangement clusters team members together while minimizing interdependence and interactive interaction with the employees outside team. The result is a close-knit group of employees who depend on one another to accomplish very difficult tasks (Mohrman, Cohen, and Mohrman 1995). The second distinctive feature of self-directed work teams is that they have substantial autonomy over the execution of their assignments. In particular, these teams plan, organize, and control work activities with little or no direct involvement of higher status authorities such as the supervisor (McShane and Von Glinow 2013). The teams are considered self-correcting because they have considerable autonomy and responsible responsibility for decisions in their work area. The third distinctive feature of self-directed teams is that they need plenty of structure. In one recent review of effective virtual teams, many of the identifying characteristics of successful teams related to creating structures such as clear operational objectives, documented work processes, and agreed-upon roles and responsibilities (Harwood 2008).

Self-directed teams are found in several industries, ranging from petrochemical plants to aircraft parts manufacturing. Most of the top-rated manufacturing firms in North America rely on self-directed teams (Panchak 2004). Indeed, self-directed teams are becoming such a popular way to organize employees in manufacturing, services, and government work that many companies do not realize they have as many self-directed teams as they do. The popularity of self-directed teams is consistent with research indicating that they potentially increase the productivity and job satisfaction. For instance, one study found that car dealer service shops that organize employees into self-directed teams are significantly more profitable than just where employees work without such a team structure (Panchak 2004). Another study reported that both short-term and long-term measures consistent with customer satisfaction increased after street cleaners in a German city were organized into self-directed work teams, which indicates that these teams are successful in nonprofit service organizations too.

The successful implementation of self-directed teams probably depends on several factors. First, self-directed teams should be responsible for the entire work process, such as making an entire product providing service. This structure keeps each team sufficiently independent from other teams yet demands a relatively high degree of interdependence among employees within the team. Self-directed teams should also have sufficient autonomy to organize and coordinate their work. Autonomy allows them to respond more quickly and effectively to client and stakeholder demands. It also motivates team members through feelings of empowerment. Finally, self-directed teams are more successful when the work site and technology support coordination and communication among team members and increase job enrichment. Too often, management calls a group of employees self-directed, yet gives the team a mandated work layout and other technologies, which isolate the employees and prevent the team's success. An additional recommendation for success in self-directed, virtual teams is that virtual team members should meet face-to-face early in the team development process. This may seem to contradict the basis of a virtual team (i.e., that they are not colocated) but no communication medium, electronic or otherwise, can produce as strong a bonding and as much initial trust as effective face-to-face interaction (Dube and Robey 2009).

It is true that all self-directed teams are not doing virtual work, but many virtual teams are self-directed teams, so there is a crossover that should be obvious here. Virtual teams, by their nature, are teams whose members operate across space, time, and organizational boundaries and are linked through information technologies to achieve organizational tasks. Virtual teams differ from traditional teams in two ways. First, they are not usually colocated, that is, they do not work in the same physical area. Second, due to the fact of their lack of colocation, members of virtual teams depend primarily on information technologies rather than face-to-face interactions communicate and coordinate their work effort. Virtual teams are an increasingly common feature in organizational life; two-thirds of human resource managers estimate that the reliance on virtual teams will grow rapidly over the next few years (McShane and Von Glinow 2013). For example, in global companies such as IBM, almost everyone in knowledge work functions as part of a virtual team. One reason why virtual teams become so widespread is new information technologies made it easier than ever before to communicate while working with people at a distance. The shift from production-based to knowledge-based work is a second reason that made virtual teamwork feasible. It is not yet possible to make a physical product when team members are located apart, but most of us now work in jobs that mainly process knowledge. Information technologies and knowledge-based work make virtual teams possible, but organizational learning and globalization should be cited as the reasons they are becoming increasingly necessary. Virtual teams represent a natural part of the organizational learning process because they encourage employees to share his knowledge where geographical limits constrain direct forms of collaboration. Globalization makes virtual teams increasingly necessary because employees are spread across the planet rather than around one building. Thus, global businesses depend on virtual teams to leverage their human capital.

Virtual teams face all the challenges of traditional teams, along with the complications arising from time and distance. Organizational behavior research is extremely interested in virtual teams, and studies are now demonstrating ways in which we can improve virtual team effectiveness. For example, members of the successful virtual teams should have particularly good information technology skills, strong self-leadership skills (i.e., as mentioned previously in the description of self-directed teams), and higher than average emotional intelligence so they can decipher the feelings of other team members from e-mails and other constrained media. Second, virtual teams should have a toolkit of communication channels, such as e-mail, virtual whiteboards, videoconferencing, and so on, as well as the freedom to choose which channel to use for each task. This may sound like an obvious suggestion, but many senior managers tend to impose technology on virtual teams, frequently based on their own opinion or advice of external consultant; thus these managers might expect virtual team members use the same communication technology throughout their work. However, research suggests that specific communication channels should be chosen as a function of the task in a level of trust operating in the virtual team at the current moment, and this choice may vary over time as the virtual team performs its work (Marlow et al. 2018). Most teams do their work on a face-to-face basis. But virtual teams use electronic technology to allow people that are in diverse physical locations to work together. They allow people to collaborate via telephone, online via video conferencing, or by e-mail. Virtual teams do things that other teams do such as make decisions, complete tasks, and share information. They can convene for a few days or for a few months to complete a project, or even exist on a somewhat permanent basis.

The three primary ways that virtual teams' communications are different from face-to-face teams' communications are: (1) the absence of para-verbal and nonverbal cues among group members, (2) limited social context, and (3) their ability to overcome time and space constraints. In a face-to-face conversation, para-verbal and nonverbal cues can be used to help clarify communications. Nonverbal cues are things like eye movements, your facial expressions, your use of hands to communicate, and other body orientation aids to language. Para-verbal cues are things like tone of voice, the inflection of your speech, and the overall volume of your voice. Virtual teams also have limited social context in that there is less direct interaction among members. Such virtual teamwork cannot duplicate in exactly the same way the give-and-take of a face-to-face discussion. Especially when members are strangers and have not personally met, virtual teams tend to be more task-oriented and exchange less social and emotional information. In other words, there is less time spent in getting to know each other. That would be one way of describing social context. Finally, there are time and space constraints are obvious in that time taken to travel to assemble meetings and to return home are avoided by virtual teams. However, more importantly work can sometimes be done asynchronously, that is, people making their contributions in different time zones and completely different times of the day. For example, Lockheed Martin, the well-known defense contractor, put together a virtual team to build a new stealth fighter plane for the U.S. military services (Crock 2003). That virtual team consisted of engineers and designers from around the globe, each of whom works in their own time zone asynchronously on a $225 billion project. The company expects this team structure to actually save $250 million over the span of a decade that it will take to create the new airplane. In other words, Lockheed Martin says that virtual teams save money as well as time.

What should a virtual team have or do to be highly effective? Well, we might break that discussion down into four parts. If a virtual team should have adequate resources, that would be our first criterion (Harwood 2008). Teams are part of a larger organization obviously and must live within the budget, policies, and practices appropriate for the entire corporation. A scarcity of resources can reduce the ability of any team and especially a virtual team to perform its job effectively. Therefore, the support group the virtual team receives from the organization includes not only the electronic media, but also timely information, proper equipment, adequate staffing, encouragement, and administrative assistants. Leadership and structure are other critical components to virtual team effectiveness. Team members must agree on who does what and ensure that all members contribute to sharing their workload. The team must decide how schedules are to be constructed, what skills need to be developed to complete the task, how the group will resolve conflicts or disagreements, and of course how the group will make and modify decisions. Leadership obviously is needed and can come in the form of a single individual or multiple individuals. On the other hand, virtual teams can also be self-directed, where team members take on many of the duties usually assigned to a manager. Virtual teams need plenty of structure; one recent review of effective virtual teams stated that many of the principles for successful virtual teams related mostly to creating those structures, such as clear operational objectives, documented work processes, and agreed-upon roles and responsibilities (Malhotra, Majchrzak, and Rosen 2007). The final recommendation is the virtual team members should meet face-to-face fairly early in the team development process. This idea may seem contradictory to the entire notion of virtual teams, but so far, no technology has replaced face-to-face interaction for producing high-level bonding and mutual understanding among virtual team members.

A review of the literature on work team effectiveness leads to the conclusion that good team communication is fundamental to team effectiveness (Marlow et al. 2016). A meta-analysis of this literature found that communication quality has a stronger predictive relationship with performance than does communication frequency. In terms of measures of communication quality, communication elaboration (i.e., the degree to which team members' sharing of information is extensive) and knowledge sharing (i.e., the extent to which team members' share their expertise and special knowledge) are most predictive of performance. This study's authors concluded that it is not communication as a whole, but instead specific elements of communication that enhance team effectiveness.

A third critical factor for virtual teams is a climate of trust members of effective teams must trust each other. Interpersonal trust among team members facilitates cooperation, reduces the need to monitor other group members' behavior, and bonds members around the belief that others on the team will not take advantage of them. Trust in leadership is also important in virtual teams, in that it allows the team to be willing to accept and commit to a leader's goals and decisions. A fourth criterion might be performance evaluation and reward systems. How do the virtual team members get rewarded and how is that individuals are held account-able for their actions? Traditionally, individually oriented evaluation and reward systems must be modified to reflect team performance within the virtual team.

In a study of 375 workers in a single high-tech company, Golden and Veiga (2008) found that supervisor and supervisee relationships were key to understanding virtual workers' organizational commitment, job satisfaction, and job performance. Their explanation for these effects is that having a higher quality relationship with your subordinates (i.e., direct reports or supervisees) is particularly important for virtual workers since their contact is mediated by technology and cues from their super-visor may be more ambiguous as a result of the technology use. Stated in a more direct way, whenever you as a manager can build high-qual-ity relationships with your virtual supervisees you will have a large and positive effect on their commitment, job satisfaction, and performance responses. Such impacts may be larger than what would be predicted for similar but face-to-face relationships. In order to improve the suc-cess of virtual teams, a number of conditions should be established. The team should have clearly defined shared objectives. In other words, the organization should take great care with the mission in charge statement of such a team. This task should be meaningful and should have some degree of complexity. Now the task can be described in a number of different terms.

Where Can Virtual Competence Be Developed?

To establish and maintain high levels of interpersonal trust among virtual workers, managers can focus on emphasizing group norms for how information should be communicated (Hoch and Kozlowski 2014; Malhotra, Majchrzak, and Rosen 2007). Virtual socializing and virtual "get-togethers" can be introduced. Use of explicit measures of team progress toward goal achievements through the use of the team's virtual workspace is recommended (Gipson and Cohen 2003; Kluemper, Mitra, and Wong 2016).

To ensure that knowledge, skills, and abilities within a virtual team are leveraged, a manager can create a skills matrix or an expertise directory that is posted asynchronously and prominently (Malhotra, Majchrzak, and Rosen 2007). Pairing diverse team members together on projects can be a means to appreciate team members' contributions (Duarte and Snyder 2001). Using asynchronous electronic bulletin boards for team members to post opinions or comments is another suggestion.

To effectively manage virtual meetings, managers can monitor team members' involvement, encouraging contributions from members who are less active, or even building "check-ins" from everyone (Malhotra, Majchrzak, and Rosen 2007). At the end of meetings, the manager should make sure the meeting notes and future work plans generated by the group are posted in some available electronic repository. Managers can also use electronic means in between meetings for facilitating idea generation or divergent thinking so that time within team meetings can be used to concentrate on idea convergence or conflict resolution.

To enhance a sense of connection to the organization, hold virtual award/reward ceremonies (Malhotra, Majchrzak, and Rosen 2007). Recognize smaller individual achievements at the start of each virtual team meeting. Make frequent report-outs to steering committees or higher authorities to enhance the external visibility of team members and ensure that these reports are known to the team members.

To avoid the responsibility trap of supervising virtual workers, encourage team member empowerment and involvement, but do not follow up that with retaining a tight control of the final decision-making or choice behaviors (Hoegl and Muethel 2016). Build shared leadership systems in problem-solving and decision-making steps all the way through to choosing final solutions.

Experts say that the specific technology or software for conducting virtual work is less important than ensuring that all team members have experience in using the technology supports. If you are unfamiliar with videoconferencing software, the best thing you can do is practice using them as the host. Modern examples of videoconferencing include such platforms as Zoom, Microsoft Teams, Google Hangouts, and GoToMeeting. See Table 5.1 for an introduction to how to schedule a Zoom meeting. If your organization uses Microsoft Teams, that package has prepared tutorials you can play to learn how to host a meeting.

Table 5.1 Basic instruction for scheduling a Zoom meeting as the meeting host

Step	Action
1	Go to the Home page
2	Click on the Schedule button a. Elect to use a passcode for privacy b. Use a waiting room to allow early arrivals to sign on c. When all participants are in the waiting room, start the meeting
3	Use the Calendar function in your organization's communications software to schedule future meetings
4	Click on Settings button a. Under *General*, select the option to have meeting controls always visible b. Under *Video*, select the option to always show participants' names on screen c. Under *Audio*, set the sound input and sound output levels for your computer d. Under *Profile*, select edit my Profile. Use a professional image for your profile photo, preferably a headshot in professional clothing

CHAPTER 6

Emotional Competence

What Is Emotional Competence?

Imagine that you come to work on a Monday morning, and you sit at your desk to begin the workday. You noticed after opening your e-mails that a request from the Human Resource Department appears asking for extensive details concerning your six employees' vacation schedules for the coming summer months. Another e-mail from Accounts Receivable demands that you provide documentation covering the training that your department received last month justifying the payment to an internal trainer who conducted the training sessions. Just then, a co-worker stops by to mention that you have an important meeting that starts in 10 minutes, and you realize that you have forgotten to read the memos necessary to prepare for that meeting. Suddenly the phone rings and it is the salesperson from a local vendor asking if you want to order office furniture to complement the office cubicle design that you chose last month for the upcoming office remodeling. As you walk to your meeting, your colleague asks, "How are you doing today?" You pause and think, wondering how you should respond to that pleasant question given your experience of the workday so far.

In terms of the language of psychology, this short example of a workday routine illustrates three different terms or concepts: affect, emotion, and mood. Affect is a term used by psychologists to refer to a variety of approach-avoidance or evaluation responses. Affect includes a broad range of feelings that people may experience, both on the job and off the job. Emotions, on the other hand, are caused by a specific event and are usually brief (i.e., lasting perhaps seconds to minutes). Emotions are usually associated with distinct facial expressions and are action-oriented in nature. Emotions can be cataloged or listed out in a taxonomy wherein specific examples might be anger, fear, happiness, or surprise. Moods are a related but conceptually different example since they are often general and diffuse, that is, they don't have a specific cause. Moods last longer than emotions, sometimes lasting for hours or maybe even over days. Moods are generally not indicated by distinct facial expressions and are in fact more cognitive in nature than emotions. Whether we consider affect, emotions, or moods, all are ideas relevant to our decision making and they are relevant to our managerial actions. To improve our management skills, we will next consider the role of emotional intelligence in our daily work lives (Mayer and Salovey 1997).

Traditional views of intelligence tend to emphasize structured verbal or mathematical learning as demonstrated by responses to academic-style problem solving (e.g., Piaget 1972; Wechsler 1939). More contemporary theories of intelligence (e.g., Gardner 1983; Sternberg 1988) argue that the traditional view is only one aspect of intelligence and that in fact there are multiple forms of intelligence. For example, Gardner (1983) saw intrapersonal intelligence as the ability to know one's own emotions, whereas interpersonal intelligence, he said, was the ability to understand another person's emotions. Emotional intelligence can be defined as everyday emotive experiences that reflect inductive or deductive reasoning and associated information processing. Emotional intelligence tells us about the individual's ability to collect, process, and effectively use emotionally relevant data in their day-to-day work lives (Frost 2004). Emotional intelligence (EQ) is one name for an individual difference factor that helps us explain the use of emotional data in management. In the mid-1990s, Daniel Goleman popularized EQ as a body of skills representing a character, which then he promoted as a means to be successful in workplace activities or management in general. Individuals, he argued, can learn to be emotionally intelligent by following his training program (Goleman 1995).

While Goleman tends to be highly positive in his description of emotional intelligence, others are less optimistic and positive about the role such a concept might play in management. In this opposing perspective, emotional intelligence is merely relabeling parts of personality as an aspect of intelligence. "There are many human virtues that are not sufficiently rewarded in our society, such as goodness and human relationships and talents in music, dance, and painting. To call them intelligence does not do justice to either theories of intelligence or to the personality traits and special talents that lie beyond the consensual definition of intelligence" (Scar 1989; p. 78).

To answer such criticism would require additional research and empirical studies. Such research would have to show that emotional intelligence can actually predict management success in terms of promotions in management positions or rated subjective evaluations of managers' behavior on the job. However, without doing a whole bunch of research, we can acknowledge that this is a popular individual difference factor and one that people see as a necessary competence in most managerial positions. Consequently, let's accept a consensus definition that has emerged on exactly what emotional intelligence is. "Emotional intelligence is the ability to monitor one's own and others' feelings and emotions, to discriminate among them and use this information to guide one's thinking and actions" (Salovey and Meyer 1989, p. 189). Within the Salovey and Meyer theoretical system, there are four components of emotional intelligence: (1) emotional perception and identification, (2) emotional facilitation, (3) emotional understanding, and (4) emotional management. Let's consider each in turn and describe what goes into those components of being an emotionally intelligent manager.

Emotional perception/identification is the ability to recognize and use input data that contain any information arising from the emotional system. It's the ability to perceive, appraise, and express emotions. So, for example, when we're dealing with an exciting and attractive option on the job, we get excited and express our enthusiasm to our co-workers. Or perhaps we recognize when we're angry and adjust our thoughts and our actions to deal with that fit of temper.

Emotional facilitation is a second factor within EQ, and it represents the ability to process emotion-laden data, such that there is an integration of cognitive factors, conscious experiences, physiological responses, and behavioral components of an emotion. So, this is essentially then recognizing what happens when we get emotional. For example, when we are frightened by the prospect of speaking in front of a group of 20 superiors describing our new project and the results to date of this new project. We might feel worried and anxious about the potential evaluation these people might make of us and we might feel flushed and hot as a physiological response, our thoughts might reflect anxiety, and we might feel nervous in the sense of having our focus and attention narrow as we begin our presentation.

A third factor is called emotional understanding, and this represents the ability to process data to assist problem solving and to improve cognitive information processing of emotion-laden data. So, an example of emotional understanding might be recognizing that we need to be evenhanded with each of our direct reports and not suppress particular approval or acceptance of one individual and while being a more judgmental or critical evaluation of everything second direct report does. Or another example might be gaining an understanding of how our own emotional state influences our decision making in some larger context.

Emotion management is the fourth factor, and it represents the ability reflecting the self-management of emotions or the management of others' emotions. This is the ability to reason between action paths and to choose among those paths directed toward the self and interacting with others. So, for example, we might choose to express frustration in front of our direct reports, but in expressing the same kind of emotional state in front of our boss or our boss's boss, we might be restrained or hide it as an inappropriate emotional expression in that context.

How Can Emotional Competence Be Assessed?

The measurement or assessment of emotional intelligence can take a variety of forms. For example, the Emotional Quotient Inventory (Bar-On 1997), contains 133 items using Likert response scales ranging from not true to very true. These items cover such things as self-awareness, self-regard, empathy, and stress tolerance. Looking at these items we would say the items look very similar to a personality trait rating form. A second type of emotional intelligence rating scale might be the Toronto Alexithymia Scale (TAS-20), which looks at a lack of emotional intelligence as an abnormal condition in a psychiatric sense (Bagby, Parker, and Taylor 1994). So, in this case, extremely low emotional intelligence is reflected in the difficulty in identifying emotions or the inability to distinguish between emotions and their associated bodily sensations or reactions. This disorder might be reflected in items where ratings show poor identification of emotions, difficulty in describing one's emotions to others, or even the existence of psychosomatic illnesses. Obviously in the case of the Toronto Alexithymia Scale, high scores demonstrate very low emotional intelligence. A third common way of measuring emotional intelligence is the Meyer, Solvay, and Caruso Emotional Intelligence Test (MSCEIT; Meyer, Solvay, and Caruso 1999). In this measurement system, a respondent is shown photographs and the respondent makes judgments about the presence or lack of motion in the photographic depictions. At second type of measurement within the MSCEIT would be to pick out among various responses to emotion-laden situations the response the respondent would be most likely to choose. For example, asking the respondent to choose the best way to cheer up another person. For our purposes, none of these forms of assessment or measurement produce accurate scores without a trained test administrator, so we will use the self-measurement rating scale that was developed by Schutte et al. (1998), which follows the Salovey and Mayer (1989) model but works as a brief self-report measure of emotional intelligence.

Self-Report Emotional Intelligence Scale

Indicate by circling the appropriate response for each item to indicate how descriptive the item is of you.

1. I know when to speak about my personal problems to others.

1	2	3	4	5
Strongly Disagree	Disagree	Neither Agree nor Disagree	Agree	Strongly Agree

2. When I am faced with obstacles, I remember times I faced similar obstacles and overcame them.

1	2	3	4	5
Strongly Disagree	Disagree	Neither Agree nor Disagree	Agree	Strongly Agree

3. I expect that I will do well on most things I try.

1	2	3	4	5
Strongly Disagree	Disagree	Neither Agree nor Disagree	Agree	Strongly Agree

4. Other people find it easy to confide in me.

1	2	3	4	5
Strongly Disagree	Disagree	Neither Agree nor Disagree	Agree	Strongly Agree

5. I find it hard to understand the nonverbal messages of other people.

5	4	3	2	1
Strongly Disagree	Disagree	Neither Agree nor Disagree	Agree	Strongly Agree

6. Some of the major events of my life have led me to reevaluate what is important and not important.

1	2	3	4	5
Strongly Disagree	Disagree	Neither Agree nor Disagree	Agree	Strongly Agree

7. When my mood changes, I see new possibilities.

1	2	3	4	5
Strongly Disagree	Disagree	Neither Agree nor Disagree	Agree	Strongly Agree

8. Emotions are one of the things that make my life worth living.

1	2	3	4	5
Strongly Disagree	Disagree	Neither Agree nor Disagree	Agree	Strongly Agree

9. I am aware of my emotions as I experience them.

1	2	3	4	5
Strongly Disagree	Disagree	Neither Agree nor Disagree	Agree	Strongly Agree

10. I expect good things to happen.

1	2	3	4	5
Strongly Disagree	Disagree	Neither Agree nor Disagree	Agree	Strongly Agree

11. I like to share my emotions with others.

1	2	3	4	5
Strongly Disagree	Disagree	Neither Agree nor Disagree	Agree	Strongly Agree

12. When I experience a positive emotion, I know how to make it last.

1	2	3	4	5
Strongly Disagree	Disagree	Neither Agree nor Disagree	Agree	Strongly Agree

13. I arrange events that others enjoy.

1	2	3	4	5
Strongly Disagree	Disagree	Neither Agree nor Disagree	Agree	Strongly Agree

14. I seek out activities that make me happy.

1	2	3	4	5
Strongly Disagree	Disagree	Neither Agree nor Disagree	Agree	Strongly Agree

15. I am aware of the nonverbal messages I send to others.

1	2	3	4	5
Strongly Disagree	Disagree	Neither Agree nor Disagree	Agree	Strongly Agree

16. I present myself in a way that makes a good impression on others.

1	2	3	4	5
Strongly Disagree	Disagree	Neither Agree nor Disagree	Agree	Strongly Agree

17. When I am in a positive mood, solving problems is easy for me.

1	2	3	4	5
Strongly Disagree	Disagree	Neither Agree nor Disagree	Agree	Strongly Agree

18. By looking at their facial expressions, I recognize the emotions people are experiencing.

1	2	3	4	5
Strongly Disagree	Disagree	Neither Agree nor Disagree	Agree	Strongly Agree

19. I know why my emotions change.

1	2	3	4	5
Strongly Disagree	Disagree	Neither Agree nor Disagree	Agree	Strongly Agree

20. When I am in a positive mood, I am able to come up with new ideas.

1	2	3	4	5
Strongly Disagree	Disagree	Neither Agree nor Disagree	Agree	Strongly Agree

21. I have control over my emotions.

1	2	3	4	5
Strongly Disagree	Disagree	Neither Agree nor Disagree	Agree	Strongly Agree

22. I easily recognize my emotions as I experience them.

1	2	3	4	5
Strongly Disagree	Disagree	Neither Agree nor Disagree	Agree	Strongly Agree

23. I motivate myself by imagining a good outcome to tasks I take on.

1	2	3	4	5
Strongly Disagree	Disagree	Neither Agree nor Disagree	Agree	Strongly Agree

24. I compliment others when they have done something well.

1	2	3	4	5
Strongly Disagree	Disagree	Neither Agree nor Disagree	Agree	Strongly Agree

25. I am aware of the nonverbal messages other people send.

1	2	3	4	5
Strongly Disagree	Disagree	Neither Agree nor Disagree	Agree	Strongly Agree

26. When another person tells me about an important event in his or her life, I almost feel as though I have experienced this event myself.

1	2	3	4	5
Strongly Disagree	Disagree	Neither Agree nor Disagree	Agree	Strongly Agree

27. When I feel a change in emotions, I tend to come up with new ideas.

1	2	3	4	5
Strongly Disagree	Disagree	Neither Agree nor Disagree	Agree	Strongly Agree

28. When I am faced with a challenge, I give up because I believe I will fail.

5	4	3	2	1
Strongly Disagree	Disagree	Neither Agree nor Disagree	Agree	Strongly Agree

29. I know what other people are feeling just by looking at them.

1	2	3	4	5
Strongly Disagree	Disagree	Neither Agree nor Disagree	Agree	Strongly Agree

30. I help other people feel better when they are down.

1	2	3	4	5
Strongly Disagree	Disagree	Neither Agree nor Disagree	Agree	Strongly Agree

31. I use good moods to help myself keep trying in the face of obstacles.

1	2	3	4	5
Strongly Disagree	Disagree	Neither Agree nor Disagree	Agree	Strongly Agree

32. I can tell how people are feeling by listening to the tone of their voice.

1	2	3	4	5
Strongly Disagree	Disagree	Neither Agree nor Disagree	Agree	Strongly Agree

33. It is difficult for me to understand why people feel the way they do.

5	4	3	2	1
Strongly Disagree	Disagree	Neither Agree nor Disagree	Agree	Strongly Agree

Scoring

Among females, the mean score is 130.94 with a standard deviation of 15.09. If you are a female and your score is 121 or lower, your score is in the lower 20 percent of all scores. If your score is 141 or higher, your score is in the upper 20 percent of all scores and you show high emotional intelligence on this scale.

Among males, the mean score is 124.78 with a standard deviation of 16.52. If you are a male and your score is 114 or lower, your score is in the lower 20 percent of all scores. If your score is 136 or higher, your score is in the upper 20 percent of all scores and you show high emotional intelligence on this scale.

Subscores	Sum Items
Perception, Appraisal and Expression of Emotion	5, 8, 9, 10, 11, 18, 19, 22, 25, 26, 29, 32, 33
Emotional Facilitation of Thinking	2, 6, 7, 17, 20, 27
Understanding, Analyzing, and Employing Emotional Knowledge	1, 3, 4, 23
Reflective Regulation of Emotions	12, 13, 14, 15, 16, 21, 24, 28, 30, 31

To compare the subscores, divide the sum of its items by the number of items in that factor to get a mean item score. Compare the mean item scores for the four factors to determine which factor is lowest, which is highest, and so on.

Why Is Emotional Competence Important in Organizations?

Individuals may want to have a valid assessment of their own emotional intelligence so that they can better set work goals and achieve better results, or they may want to have such an assessment so that they may better understand problems they have experienced interpersonally or even intrapersonally (e.g., gaining insight into to their own levels of impulse control). But perhaps the best reason to have this type of intelligence measured is to use that self-insight when entering into workplaces or work tasks that challenge that type of intelligence (Schutte et al. 1998).

Some authors have argued for the importance of possessing emotional intelligence for everyday life concerns and state that is valuable in many domains (Bar-On and Packer 2000; Ciarrochi, Forgas, and Mayer 2001; Mayer and Salovey 1997). Cooper (1997) believes that higher levels of emotional intelligence create life success by allowing for greater career success, leading to stronger personal relationships, providing for more leadership skills, being associated with more energy and health, and predicting better performance in high-pressure situations in life. In terms of job performance, Law, Wong, and Song (2004) reported a large-scale field study of factory workers' job performance as predicted by emotional intelligence and the Big Five Personality Factors (i.e., Introversion–Extraversion, Neuroticism, Openness to Experience, Agreeableness, and Conscientiousness). These researchers found that emotional intelligence predicted measures of task performance, job involvement, and organizational citizenship beyond any predictive power based on the Big Five Personality measures. This was taken as evidence for emotional intelligence being different from personality traits and as evidence that emotional intelligence predicts multiple measures of job outcomes.

There have been several important review and summary articles on the impact of emotional intelligence in the workplace. Cherniss (2004) reviewed empirical data studies and concluded that emotional intelligence is a predictor of job performance in such occupations as military recruiters, sales personnel, mechanics, business consultants, global multinational executives, manufacturing supervisors, retail store managers, debt collectors, and financial advisors employed by American Express. Van Rooy and Viswesvaran (2004) conducted a meta-analysis of 59 empirical studies of emotional intelligence and job performance and their conclusion was that emotional intelligence correlated moderately ($r = +.24$) with measures of job performance in the reviewed studies. When these authors broke down emotional intelligence into components that are most connected with problem solving (i.e., assimilation of emotional information into one's own cognitions and understanding for what causes various emotions), they found the best evidence for the prediction of job performance. When the authors look at the components that are most relevant to others' emotional states (i.e., perception of others' emotions and management of others' emotional behaviors), they found weaker prediction for job performance measures (e.g., correlations from +.13 to +.19). Their conclusion was that the best use of emotional intelligence in work settings was found in empathizing with co-workers and in working together with co-workers to achieve productivity. O'Boyle et al. (2011) also conducted a meta-analytic study of emotional intelligence studies. In this case, the researchers were directly comparing measures of emotional intelligence with measures of cognitive ability and the Big Five Personality traits. This is a valuable assessment of emotional intelligence's independent and significant predictive power when considered in comparison to other common selection and promotion measures. They concluded that emotional intelligence added 13.2 percent to the total variance in job performance accounted for by the entire set of predictors and that while cognitive ability was the best type of predictor, emotional intelligence was the next best predictor, and that personality factors were less effective than either cognitive ability or emotional intelligence. Joseph et al. (2015) found similar results for the comparison to cognitive ability and personality measures but examined how emotional intelligence was measured. These researchers found that the more closely emotional intelligence was defined in terms of abilities, the better those measures predicted job performance outcomes. What some experts call mixed-model definitions for emotional intelligence (i.e., mixed models include traits and values along with abilities) were found to be less clearly linked to job performance. This aligns with other critiques of emotional intelligence as being too broadly defined (Conte 2005; Decker 2003; Locke 2005). If the two views of ability, that is of cognitive ability and emotional abilities, are directly compared, researchers have found that emotional intelligence becomes increasingly important as a predictor when cognitive abilities decline in their ability to predict job outcomes (Cote and Miners 2006). For example, when job performance is defined as organizational citizenship, emotional intelligence is a good predictor of citizenship behaviors as indicated by promoting the image or reputation of the employing organization. If citizenship is defined as assisting others with their job tasks, then cognitive abilities remain the single best predictor of those type of outcomes.

A more specific question to be addressed is how well emotional intelligence predicts performance in managerial roles. Rosete and Ciarrochi (2005) looked at a sample of 41 senior business executives and found a positive correlation for their emotional intelligence abilities with their job performance measures. In a very large field study within a manufacturing organization (i.e., managers were studied who collectively supervised over 1,200 employees), researchers reported that intrapersonal measures of emotional intelligence predicted overall leadership effectiveness (Kerr et al. 2005). What is interesting in this study is that measures similar to the constructs of the Mayer-Salovey-Caruso Emotional Intelligence Test (i.e., the four-factor definition of emotional intelligence as abilities) were completed as ratings from the managers' subordinates or direct reports. In this empirical study, emotional intelligence measures accounted for 15.2 percent of the variance in leadership effectiveness ratings. Elfenbein and Ambady (2002) discussed emotional intelligence among managers as the ability to recognize emotions in others' facial expressions, which these others describe as a nonverbal "eavesdrop" ability for managers to rely upon. In this study, recognition of emotional cues was predictive of ratings for the managers' value to their organization. Chien Farh, Seo, and Tesluk (2012) claim that the reason emotional intelligence among managers predicts their performance in promoting teamwork effectiveness lies in it promoting managers' responses to co-workers' salient emotion-laden cues, which in turn activates co-workers' emotional capabilities. Their argument is that managers of work teams perform emotional labor in that they respond to co-workers' expressions of emotion by channeling the emotional responses of others into productive work efforts. This might mean, for example, that a manager learns to deal with negative expressions of emotion among direct reports as well as their positive emotions and that in either case emotional energy is reacted to and channeled in ways that lead to greater work results. The effective manager learns to use their abilities to identify emotions, think constructively about emotions, empathize with others' emotions, and to guide and direct others' actions in emotion-based activities in ways that are productive (Humphrey 2002).

Emotionally intelligent managers can promote effectiveness at all levels of an organization (George 2000), which means that emotional intelligence measures the extent to which a person's cognitive capabilities are informed by emotional data and the extent to which emotions in one-self and others are cognitively managed. George proposes five means by which emotional intelligence affects managerial effectiveness:

1. It aids a manager directing the development of collective goals.
2. It causes others to appreciate the importance of work tasks.
3. It helps generate and maintain enthusiasm and confidence among co-workers.
4. It encourages flexibility in decision making.
5. It helps the manager to facilitate other's internalization of organizational goals and values.

Others have argued that emotional intelligence predicts the occurrence of specific leadership behaviors and leadership emergence in self-directed work teams (Caruso, Mayer, and Salovey 2002; Walter, Humphrey, and Cole 2012). They stress, however, that emotional intelligence's broad impacts on management and teamwork reflects skill and ability development more that surface learning or the use of social masks. Joseph and Newman (2010) argued that those learning emotional intelligence should follow a cascading skill-building model such that perception of emotions is the most basic skill, followed by understanding of the causes and consequences of emotions, then followed by the regulation of emotional thought and judgment, and then that the final level of learning involved performance and management of self and others' emotional responses and behaviors. Regarding this final learning step, some researchers (Austin et al. 2007) have investigated whether emotional intelligence is simply cynical manipulation in the same manner of Machiavellianism. Their results indicate that emotional intelligence is not the same as emotional manipulation of others. You can rest assured that increasing your emotional abilities will not mean giving in to the "dark side" of management.

Opposing pairs of basic emotions

Joy..Sadness

Admiration...Loathing

Fear...Anger

Interest..Distraction

Figure 6.1 Opposing pairs of basic emotions

Where Can Emotional Competence Be Developed?

To develop your ability to identify emotions, begin keeping a journal or diary of emotions identified in co-workers. Use the opposing pairs of emotions shown in Figure 6.1 as a guide for what to look for in others' expressions. Keep in mind that basic emotions are expressed in both verbal ways, in para-verbal ways (e.g., volume or loudness of voice), and in non-verbal ways (e.g., how hand and arm gestures occur). Keep your records by noting the type of emotion, any facial expressions, the body language, the tone of voice, and the emotional responses (i.e., both behavioral and cognitive) for each entry. Don't limit your observations to the emotions listed in Figure 6.1 but use those as a starting point. Add observations of yourself as you become more familiar with the method.

To develop your ability to use emotions to facilitate thinking, document any significant decisions in your department over the period of two months. Map any emotional cues you notice as they appear relevant at the time and then also at the end of the two months, return to each entry and note any emotional cues that hindsight or retrospective review affords you.

To develop your ability to understand and empathize with others' emotions, ask co-workers for their experiences that they feel illustrate emotional aspects of their jobs. These "emotional stories" should be recorded (e.g., you could use the audio-recording function on your smartphone and/or take notes by writing things down) for later analysis. Map out the causes and consequences of emotional episodes you collect by noting the triggering events, the cognitive responses, the subjective

Table 6.1 Mapping the causes and consequences of emotional states

Preceding event	Cognition	Emotion	Behavior	Consequence
Threat	Danger	Fear	Escape	Safety
Obstacle	Enemy	Anger	Attack	Removal
Perception of potential reward	Possession	Joy	Acquisition	Increased outcomes
Perception of loss of a reward	Abandonment	Sadness	Depressed activities	Rumination on lost outcomes
Assigned co-worker	Possible friend	Acceptance	Socializing	Supportive ally
New Task	Examine	Expectation	Plan	Develop or extend knowledge
Unexpected assignment	Explore	Surprise	Halt current activity	Seek time to orient

or feeling responses, the behavioral responses, and the effects or consequences of all the responses. You can use Table 6.1 as a guide for how to construct these maps.

To develop your ability to manage emotions, ask your mentor for coaching regarding how they manage their own or co-workers' emotions. In this instruction, pay particular attention to what is responded to directly, what should be responded to indirectly, and what is not responded to at all. Be sensitive to vertical power relationships as they come up in the instruction by being aware if the other person is a superior, a peer, or a subordinate in the formal authority hierarchy of your organization.

CHAPTER 7

Cross-Cultural Competence

What Is Cross-Cultural Competence?

The word "culture" comes from the Latin word *cultura*, which refers to the idea of a cult or worship, and thus this term refers to the result of human interaction (Joynt and Warner 1996). Culture can be defined in its modern usage as acquired knowledge that people use to interpret their experiences and then use that knowledge to generate rules for social behavior. This knowledge is the basis for values, helps create attitudes, and ultimately influences people's behavior. Most scholars of culture would agree on the following characteristics of culture (Luthans and Doh 2015). First, culture is neither inherited nor biologically based but acquired by learning and experience. Second, individuals as members of a group, an organization, or a society share its culture. Therefore, culture is not specific to single individuals or to small groups. Third, culture is transmitted across generations and is cumulative. In other words, it is passed down from one generation to the next as rules for how to live well. Fourth, culture is based on human abilities to symbolize elements of their experiences in abstract or generalized symbols. In this way then culture allows us to represent one thing by another. Fifth, culture provides structure to the human experience and integrates our perceptions into a pattern. Culture then gives us a cohesive structure so that we can predict if a change occurs in one area how that change will affect behavior values or experiences in another part of life. Sixth, culture is based on the fact that humans have the capability of adaptation, that is, it helps us learn to change as needed.

Many different cultures exist around the world, which means that understanding the impact of culture on organizational behavior is critical for studying international business practices. If managers do not know something about the culture of the people in the country they do business with, then the results of that lack of information can be quite disastrous in a business sense. Even without direct business contacts in a different culture, understanding of and reacting to cultural differences appropriately is increasingly important throughout business as globalism becomes the dominant theme and more and more cultures become interconnected. Consequently, researchers have attempted to provide a composite picture of how culture influences business organizations. In 1980, a Dutch researcher named Gert Hofstede identified four universal dimensions of culture relevant to business and later added two more in an attempt to explain how culture influences what people do in their work lives. The data were gathered from surveys conducted with 116,000 respondents from 70 different countries around the world, all of whom worked at branches of IBM (Hofstede 1980; House et al. 2004). The fact that they all worked for one company has been used as a criticism of the global study. However, Hofstede felt strongly that IBM employees are special people and because they all worked for IBM and had similar education and knowledge of certain technical aspects of the software and electronics business, they had professional and occupational interests in common. Variation due to their culture, then, can be directly compared because cultural differences from their society would stand out better. Over the past 40 years, many people have found great value in the Hofstede study and the fact that it comes from a single organization emerges, then, as a strength. The four original dimensions will be described next.

Power distance is the extent to which less powerful members of institutions and organizations accept that power is distributed unequally within their firm. Individuals living in countries where employees obey without question the orders of their superiors live in a culture with high power distance. These employees tend to follow orders as a matter of procedure without question and strict obedience to authority is found even at the upper levels of management. Examples of high-power cultures would include Mexico, South Korea, and India. The effects of this dimension can be measured in a number of ways. One way would be to look at how power distance relates to organizational design. Organizations and cultures that have low power distance tend to be decentralized and have flatter organizational structures. On the other hand, organizations in high power distance cultures tend to look more centralized and have taller or more elaborate organizational authority hierarchies. Looking at it in terms of organizational size and supervisory personnel, cultures with a high power distance tend to have relatively large number of managers compared to those in low power distance cultures. To put it simply, high-power distance encourages and promotes obvious differences in status between people at different levels of management. See Table 7.1 for examples of countries scoring high and low on these values.

Uncertainty avoidance is the extent to which people feel threatened by ambiguous situations and hold beliefs and act in ways to avoid ambiguous situations. High uncertainty avoidance cultures also tend to show a high need for security and a strong belief in experts and their knowledge. Examples of high uncertainty avoidance cultures would include Germany, Japan, and Spain. Cultures with low uncertainty avoidance have people who are more willing to accept the risk associated with the unknown and to feel greater comfort with socially ambiguous situations. The effects of uncertainty avoidance can be measured in a number of ways. High uncertainty avoidance cultures tend to structure their organizational activities formally, they have more written rules, their managers generally avoid taking risks, there usually is lower labor turnover in such cultures, and employees on the whole tend to be less ambitious. Low uncertainty avoidance cultures, then, would be described in the opposite terms such that an organization in such a culture would encourage personnel to use their

Table 7.1 Countries representing extreme scores on four universal cultural dimensions

Cultural dimension	Highest ranking countries	Lowest ranking countries
Power distance	Mexico South Korea India	Austria New Zealand Israel
Uncertainty avoidance	Russia France Greece	Denmark United Kingdom Singapore
Individualism	United States Australia Italy	Venezuela China Nigeria
Masculinity	Japan Germany South Africa	Sweden Costa Rica Thailand

own initiative and assume personal responsibility for their actions and to show more risk-taking among their managers. Countries with lower power distance cultures include Austria, New Zealand, and Israel.

Individualism is the tendency for people to look after themselves and their immediate family primary duty. The opposite of individualism is called collectivism. Collectivism is the tendency of people to bond to groups or collectives and to look at other group members for support and care in exchange for loyalty to the group as a whole. The United States, Australia, and Italy are examples of a high individualism countries. Collectivism is relatively stronger in places such as Venezuela, Nigeria, and China. Countries with high individualism tend to have beliefs that reflect the Protestant work ethic, the employees in such cultures show greater individual initiative in work organizations, and job promotions tend to be based on the market value of the position. Countries with a low individualism, that is, countries more characterized by collectivism, tend to have less support for the Protestant work ethic belief system, individuals in these cultures show less initiative, and job promotions tend to be based more on seniority.

Masculinity is defined as a situation in which dominant values and society are characterized as seeking success, money, and things. The opposite or opposing end of the continuum of masculinity is femininity. Hofstede described femininity as a situation in which the dominant values in the society are caring for others and ensuring the quality of life. Countries with a high masculinity score (e.g., Japan, Germany, and South Africa) place greater importance on earnings, recognition, advancement, and challenge. Individuals in such a culture are encouraged be independent decision makers and to strive for personal achievements. Personal success is thought to be reflected in the individual's social recognition and personal wealth. The workplace is often characterized by high job stress and many managers believe that their employees dislike work and must be kept under some degree of control by the organization and its supervisors. Countries with low masculinity, that is, with a higher score on femininity, tend to place greater importance on cooperation, a friendly working atmosphere, and employment security. An example of such a culture might be Sweden where individuals are encouraged to be group decision makers and achievement is defined in terms of the creation of a positive living environment. In work organizations in a high femininity culture, the workplace tends to be characterized as having a less job-related stress, and managers tend to give their employees more credit for being responsible and allow them greater freedom at work.

Two additional cultural dimensions were added later by Hofstede, one being a dimension extending from universalism at one end to particularism at the other end, and a second dimension with achievement at one extreme and description anchoring the other extreme (Trompenaars and Hampden-Turner 1998). Universalism versus particularism is described as a distinction between the belief that ideas and practices can be applied everywhere without modification, whereas particularism is the belief that circumstances dictate how ideas and practices should be applied. Cultures with high universalism values tend to focus more on formal rules than on relationships and follow business contracts very closely, believing that contractual relationships are very binding. The cultures with high particularism instead focus more on relationships and established personal trust rather than on formal rules or contracts. In a particularism culture, legal contracts are frequently modified, it is assumed that the parties involved will get to know each other better, that personal bonds are more binding than legal language in a contract. The United States, Australia, and Germany would be examples of high universalism cultures whereas countries such as Venezuela, Russia, and China are high on particularism.

Achievement cultures are cultures in which people are accorded status based on how well they perform their functions. At the other end of this dimension are description cultures. A description culture is the one in which status is based on who the person is or what their title or name might be. Achievement cultures give high status to high achievers, such as the company's number one salesperson or medical researcher who has found a cure for an important disease. Description cultures accord status based on age, gender, or social connections. For example, in a description culture, an employee who's been with the company for 40 years may be listened to carefully by other employees because of the respect that others have for that individual's age and seniority. In description cultures, employees may have status due to their personal connections so that in China, for example, an employee who is Communist Party member may be afforded status because of whom she knows. The United States, Austria, and United Kingdom would be examples of achievement cultures and Venezuela, Indonesia, and China are examples of description cultures.

Time is yet another dimension that demonstrates major cultural differences. One continuum related to time is the sequential time orientation versus the asynchronous time orientation. In cultures where sequential approaches are prevalent, people tend to do only one activity at a time, they believe in keeping appointments strictly, and they show a strong preference for following plans as they are laid out and not deviating from them. In cultures where asynchronous approaches are common, people tend to do more than one activity at a time, appointments are more proximate and may be changed at a moment's notice, and work schedules generally are less important than relationships. People in asynchronous time cultures often stop what they are doing to meet and greet individuals that come into contact during that work period. The United States would be a good example of a sequential time orientation, and Mexico would be a good example of an asynchronous time orientation. In a related vein, cultures can also be past or present oriented as opposed to future oriented. For instance, in the United States, the future is more important than the past or the present. In countries such as Venezuela or Spain, however, the present is more important. Thus, doing business in future-oriented cultures, managers should emphasize opportunities and the limits to any agreement, agree to specific deadlines for getting things done, and be aware of core competencies that the other party needs to implement. When doing business with past- or present-oriented cultures, a manager should emphasize history and the tradition of business practices, find out whether internal relationships must approve the types of changes that are needed, and agree to future meetings in principle but consider them flexible. Clearly, in such cultures, deadlines for project completion are not fixed.

The GLOBE project was what IBM called their study of culture's consequences and it set out to answer many fundamental questions about how cultural variables affect organizational life (House et al. 2004). An overarching goal of the GLOBE project was to develop correctly based ideas that could be used to describe, understand, and predict the impact of various cultural variables on management and effectiveness of management in many different industries. The project hoped to provide universal standards and guidelines that allowed managers to focus on local specialization and practices. Three fundamental questions were addressed by the project. One, are there leader behaviors, attributes, and organizational practices that are universally accepted and effective across all cultures? Two, are there leader behaviors, attributes, and organizational practices that are accepted and are effective in only specific cultures? Three, can attributes of societal culture affect the kinds of organizational changes or business initiatives that will be accepted and will be effective in the future? We will return to these questions when we discuss the importance of cross-culture competency later.

How Can Cultural Competence Be Assessed?

A self-report measure of cultural intelligence was developed recently (Ang, Van Dyne, and Koh 2004; Ang, Van Dyne, and Koh 2006; Fischer, Lam, and Hall 2009). The intent of the measure is to get a self-assessment of attitudes and behaviors relevant to interacting with other cultures.

The Cultural Intelligence Scale

Read each statement and select the response that best describes your capabilities. Select the answer that *best* describes you *as you really are.*

1. I am conscious of the cultural knowledge I use when interacting with people with different cultural backgrounds.

1	2	3	4	5
Strongly Disagree	Disagree	Neither Agree nor Disagree	Agree	Strongly Agree

2. I know the legal and economic systems of other cultures.

1	2	3	4	5
Strongly Disagree	Disagree	Neither Agree nor Disagree	Agree	Strongly Agree

3. I enjoy interacting with people from different cultures.

1	2	3	4	5
Strongly Disagree	Disagree	Neither Agree nor Disagree	Agree	Strongly Agree

4. I change my verbal behavior (e.g., accent and tone) when a cross-cultural interaction requires it.

1	2	3	4	5
Strongly Disagree	Disagree	Neither Agree nor Disagree	Agree	Strongly Agree

5. I adjust my cultural knowledge as I interact with people from a culture that is unfamiliar to me.

1	2	3	4	5
Strongly Disagree	Disagree	Neither Agree nor Disagree	Agree	Strongly Agree

6. I know the rules (e.g., vocabulary and grammar) of other languages.

1	2	3	4	5
Strongly Disagree	Disagree	Neither Agree nor Disagree	Agree	Strongly Agree

7. I am confident that I can socialize with locals in a culture that is unfamiliar to me.

1	2	3	4	5
Strongly Disagree	Disagree	Neither Agree nor Disagree	Agree	Strongly Agree

8. I use pause and silence differently to suit different cross-cultural situations.

1	2	3	4	5
Strongly Disagree	Disagree	Neither Agree nor Disagree	Agree	Strongly Agree

9. I am conscious of the cultural knowledge I apply to cross-cultural interactions.

1	2	3	4	5
Strongly Disagree	Disagree	Neither Agree nor Disagree	Agree	Strongly Agree

10. I know the cultural values and religious beliefs of other cultures.

1	2	3	4	5
Strongly Disagree	Disagree	Neither Agree nor Disagree	Agree	Strongly Agree

11. I am sure I can deal with the stresses of adjusting to a culture that is new to me.

1	2	3	4	5
Strongly Disagree	Disagree	Neither Agree nor Disagree	Agree	Strongly Agree

12. I vary the rate of my speaking when a cross-cultural situation requires it.

1	2	3	4	5
Strongly Disagree	Disagree	Neither Agree nor Disagree	Agree	Strongly Agree

13. I check the accuracy of my cultural knowledge as I interact with people from different cultures.

1	2	3	4	5
Strongly Disagree	Disagree	Neither Agree nor Disagree	Agree	Strongly Agree

14. I know the marriage systems of other cultures.

1	2	3	4	5
Strongly Disagree	Disagree	Neither Agree nor Disagree	Agree	Strongly Agree

15. I enjoy living in cultures that are unfamiliar to me.

1	2	3	4	5
Strongly Disagree	Disagree	Neither Agree nor Disagree	Agree	Strongly Agree

16. I change my nonverbal behavior when a cross-cultural situation requires it.

1	2	3	4	5
Strongly Disagree	Disagree	Neither Agree nor Disagree	Agree	Strongly Agree

17. I know the arts and crafts of other cultures.

1	2	3	4	5
Strongly Disagree	Disagree	Neither Agree nor Disagree	Agree	Strongly Agree

18. I am confident that I can get accustomed to the shopping conditions in a different culture.

1	2	3	4	5
Strongly Disagree	Disagree	Neither Agree nor Disagree	Agree	Strongly Agree

19. I alter my facial expressions when a cross-cultural interaction requires it.

1	2	3	4	5
Strongly Disagree	Disagree	Neither Agree nor Disagree	Agree	Strongly Agree

20. I know the rules for expressing nonverbal behaviors in other cultures.

1	2	3	4	5
Strongly Disagree	Disagree	Neither Agree nor Disagree	Agree	Strongly Agree

Scoring

Metacognitive Cultural Intelligence (Sum items 1, 5, 9, 13)
Scores less than 14 are low, between 15 and 17 are moderate, and greater than 18 are high

Cognitive Cultural Intelligence (Sum items 2, 6, 10, 14, 17, 20)
Scores less than 16 are low, between 17 and 25 are moderate, and greater than 26 are high
Motivational Cultural Intelligence (Sum items 3, 7, 11, 15, 18)
Scores less than 16 are low, between 17 and 21 are moderate, and greater than 22 are high
Behavioral Cultural Intelligence (Sum items 4, 6, 8, 16, 19)
Scores less than 16 are low, between 17 and 21 are moderate, and greater than 22 are high

Why Is Cross-Cultural Competence Important in Organizations?

Before considering the importance of cross-cultural competence for individual managers within a corporation, let us first look at how entire multinational corporations orient themselves toward cultural differences. Multinational corporations are grounded in the belief that a worldwide approach to doing business is fundamental to achieving efficiency and effectiveness. These organizations respond to the imperatives of globalization in a variety of ways. Taking advertising as a good example of responding to national preferences, we see in the United Kingdom that consumers value laughter, and popular ads that feature a broad and self-deprecating humor aimed at both the advertiser and the consumer are the most effective ads. (Hoecklin 1995). In France, however, advertising is primarily emotional and symbolic with ads constructed without reliance on logic or reason. Think of an ad as a cultural event in France. In Germany, the public wants factual and rational advertising with appeals to problem solving and choice. Just this short example makes clear that globalization makes managing difficult across boundaries due to local customers demanding differentiated appeals. Related to these points but more indirectly are factors like consumer preferences for buying "local" and the diversity of worldwide industry standards. To succeed as global enterprises, multinationals should avoid parochialism and simplification. Parochialism in international business means to view the world through the perspective of the company's home culture. Simplification in international business would mean relying on the same orientation to business even when dealing with significantly different cultural groups.

It is fair to conclude that there are far more known and researched cultural differences than similarities in the cross-cultural study of management. It is clear, for example, that cultural differences are common in wages, other types of compensation, pay equity, maternity/paternity leaves granted, and the importance of specific criteria used in the evaluation of employees (Tsai, 2011). If we use the Project Globe emic (i.e., true in all cultures) dimensions of cultural values relevant to business to compare countries such as Japan, Germany, Mexico, and China (Hofstede, Hofstede, and Minkov, 2005), we see some variations important to managing employees in these different local markets (see Table 7.2). In Japan, high masculinity and uncertainty avoidance means highly assertive but clearly structured management is preferred. Also, within Asia, in China uncertainty avoidance is low but power distance is high, so managers need not clarify and structure directions but instead rely on organizational powers and the authority of their legitimized roles. Mexico, in North America, is also high on power distance like China but is also high on masculinity and uncertainty avoidance, like Japan. Of course, Germany, like the United States, is high on individualism. In Table 7.3, implications for human resource management practices within a multinational corporation choosing to operate within each of these national markets are indicated. Hiring practices in Japan, for example, must reflect the kind of long-term nature of employment bonds assumed in that culture. In Germany, all skilled labor positions must be filled by relying on the local apprenticeship programs and in China hiring should be sensitive to the recent changes in public policy that impact hiring decisions. Most extreme in impact would be Mexico,

Table 7.2 Comparing for different national markets on four common dimensions of corporate culture

Country	Power distance	Individualism	Masculinity	Uncertainty avoidance
Japan	Moderate	Moderate	High	High
Germany	Low	High	Moderate	Moderate
Mexico	High	Low	High	High
China	High	Low	Moderate	Low

Table 7.3 Suggested HRM practices for subsidiaries located in Japan, Germany, Mexico, and China

HR practice	Japan	Germany	Mexico	China
Recruitment and selection	-Prepare for long hiring processes -Develop trusting relationships with potential hires -Ensure your firm is perceived as "here-to-stay"	-Obtained all skilled labor from government-subsidized apprenticeship programs	-Use expatriates sparingly -Recruit Mexican nationals at U.S. universities	-Use local selection processes as established recently by public policy initiatives
Training	-Invest substantially in training -Adopt general training and cross-training -Ensure all organizational units and levels of management are involved in training	-Adapt training to build on local apprenticeship training -Be mindful of governmental regulations for training	-Use bilingual trainers	-Use team-based training wherever possible
Compensation	-Use public recognition and praise as a principal motivator -Avoid pay for performance plans as incentives	-Adjust for high labor costs for manufacturing	-Consider all aspects of labor costs in adjusting compensation plans	-Use technical training as a reward -Recognize egalitarian values in creating incentives -Avoid over-reliance on overtime and "more work, more pay" plans

where multinationals are strongly encouraged to avoid expatriate assignments from the home country and instead to rely on home country hires.

If a multinational operates in China, international business experts (Chen 2001; Conlin 2007; Harris and Moran 1991) recommend the following seven points:

1. Recognize the higher value the Chinese place on values and principles above money.

2. Assume that business meetings must begin with tea and social pleasantries.

3. Wait for the Chinese host to signal when the business portion of the meeting begins.

4. The Chinese slowly formulate action plans, but once made they commit and stay with plans.

5. In negotiations, reciprocity is key. If a concession is given, one is expected in return.

6. Negotiations are commonly conducted through intermediaries to avoid any possible direct loss of face and for similar reasons, any show of strong emotions (e.g., anger or frustration) will be viewed as unseemly.

7. Negotiations should always be viewed as an investment in a long-term relationship.

Similar lists can be made regarding the other countries in the previous tables; however, China is listed here only as an example for how cultures can vary on their views of human nature and how that in consequence has a large impact on business practices. Kluckhohn and Strodbeck (1961) helped to summarize cultural variation in viewing basic human values by making six comparisons:

1. What is the nature of humanity? Responses range from good to evil.

2. What is humanity's orientation toward nature? Responses range from subjugation to in harmony with nature to domination.

3. What is the basis for interpersonal relationships? Responses range from hierarchical to collectivist to individualistic.

4. What is humanity's basic mode of expression? Responses range from being to doing.

5. What is humanity's time orientation? Responses range from past to present to future.

6. What is humanity's view of social space? Responses range from private to public.

Each culture has its own responses to these six perspectives. In the United States, the responses, in order, would be: a mixture of good and evil, dominant, individualistic, doing, future, and private.

Multinational corporations position themselves toward operating in different cultural milieus in one of four strategic ways: ethnocentric, polycentric, regiocentric, and geocentric (Chakravarthy and Perlmutter 1985). The ethnocentric strategic predisposition is the original overseas strategy of an imperialistic culture in that it demonstrates a nationalistic philosophy of management whereby the values and interests of the parent company guide the corporation's strategic decisions overseas. In the polycentric predisposition, strategic decisions are tailored to suit the culture of the countries where the multinational corporation operates. Each is potentially unique in the case of polycentric. In the discussion comparing Japan, Germany, Mexico, and China, if a corporation were to follow those implications, it would be implementing a polycentric orientation. However, the Kluckhohn and Strodbeck (1961) core values argument could lead a corporation to pursue groups of cultures that follow similar perspectives. In the regiocentric orientation, the organization attempts to blend its own interests with those of the subsidiary organizations on a regional basis. For example, European operations might be blended in one fashion while operations in Asia would be blended with company's interests in a different way. Finally, there is the geocentric orientation, which reflects an attempt by the company to integrate into its decision making a global systems approach. Table 7.4 takes these four global business approaches and outlines how they might impact corporate strategy, design, culture, and then finally human resources practices. The overall conclusion from considering this table might be that a firm need not feel that they must "reinvent the wheel" when deciding to become a multinational.

One area the culturally competent manager should be concerned about in gaining an understanding of cultural differences is work motivation. The psychological basis for understanding motivation is seeing it as a process by which unsatisfied wants or needs create intentions and actions, which business professionals hope to channel toward meeting goals and objectives. This assumes that work motivation can be a content theory, wherein what arouses, energizes, or initiates employee behavior typically causes a manager to focus on employees' personal characteristics. But this statement also can be interpreted to say that motivation is a process in which how employees' behaviors and intentions are channeled,

Table 7.4 Four global business approaches and their implications for strategy, organizational design and culture, and human resources practices

	Ethnocentric	Polycentric	Regiocentric	Geocentric
Rationale for corporate strategy	Global integration	National responsiveness	Regional integration and national respon-siveness	Global integration and national responsiveness
Typical organization design	Hierarchical product divisions	Hierarchical area divisions	Product and regional divi-sions tied via a matrix	Boundaryless network of organizations
Source of corporate culture	Home country	Host country	Regional	Global
Human resources practices	Home country staff developed for positions worldwide	Staff from local national-ity developed for key posi-tions locally	Regional staff developed for key positions regionally	Best staff anywhere developed for key positions everywhere

redirected, or even halted. Motivation as a process is more likely to help the manager see how the individual interacts with their current situation. The knowledge of work motivation can be divided as well by seeing motivation as intrinsic or extrinsic. If motivation is intrinsically controlled, then the individual worker's experience of involvement or fulfillment spur on their activity. If the work motivation is controlled by extrinsic or external environmental factors, then that will lead the culturally competent manager to study incentives, competition, and compensation plans.

We can focus on one well-known theory to examine the balance between intrinsic and extrinsic controls at the same time as examining cultural differences. Maslow's hierarchy of needs theory posits that five basic needs constitute a hierarchy of motives that operate like a stage theory (Maslow 1943). The needs are ordered from most fundamental to more advanced or higher order. The five needs are physiological (e.g., physical needs for food, clothing, and shelter), safety (e.g., security, sta-bility, and freedom from pain), social (e.g., needs to interact with and feel wanted by others), esteem (e.g., needs for power and status), and self-actualization (e.g., needs to reach full human potential). The theory adds the principle of satisfaction-progression to the five need types and so this means a person seeks satisfaction of the most fundamental needs first and progresses onward toward satisfying higher order needs after initial need types are satisfied (i.e., a satisfied need no longer motivates the work behavior). The other major principle in this theory is frustration-regression, which means that frustration at a higher order need type will lead to regression to a lower order need (i.e., it once again will predominate or focus one's attention for satisfaction). We can use this popular theory to question whether work motivation theories are universal, meaning that people in all cultures are motivated by similar content and influenced by similar motivational processes (Mead 1994). Or we can investigate the particularistic assumptions of work motivation, saying that individuals in two cultures may vary in motivational content, or they may vary in how motivational processes operate, or in fact both motive content and motivational process are specific to individual societal cultures.

International studies of Maslow's need hierarchy as a theory of work motivation have found that managers indicate that higher order needs are most important to them and that autonomy and self-actualization needs were most important and least satisfied needs among managers in North American and European organizations whereas nonmanagement workers in manufacturing plants felt that physiological and safety needs were most important (Hofstede 1972). These findings support the universalistic perspective mentioned earlier. But it is also true that in Asian cultures evidence for only four types of needs were found (i.e., from lower order to higher order the needs were social, physiological, safety, and self-actualization) and that self-actualization needs referred more to being in the service of society than to fulfilling one's own human potential (Gambrel and Cianci 2003). This supports the specific cultural perspective.

Job design and quality of work life are two applications of work motivation that are popular and have been studied internationally (Haire, Ghiselli, and Porter 1966). These programs can be concerned with both motivational content and process. Overall, it seems that the impact of these programs does vary by the culture of the country in which they are applied. Factory workers in Japan feel they must work for many hours at a rapid pace and have little control over their work activities. Similar workers in Sweden see their work as having a more relaxed pace and see themselves as having a great deal of control over their work activities. U.S. workers in similar settings fall in between these two, and they report having a less demanding pace than the Japanese but also see their work as less self-controlled than the Swedes. International research on work centrality, a concept linked to overall quality of work life perceptions, has found that workers in the UK have low levels of centrality, workers in Germany and the Netherlands have moderately low levels, U.S. workers have moderate levels, and workers in Japan report the highest levels (Bhagat et al. 1990). In terms of work process factors, the conclusions are that American and Japanese workers are willing to work long hours because of the cost of living in those cultures is high. In Japan, for example, salaried employees aren't paid extra to work late, but cultural expectations are that they should be willing to do so. Some argue that these long hours may reflect work socializing time (e.g., obligations to hang out with the boss and co-workers) more than it reflects on-task activities (Luthans and Doh 2015). In Japan, excessive hours and job burnout has a name, *karoshi*, and is recognized as a social problem (Bhagat, Segovis, and Nelson 2016).

Work-related communications are frequently clustered and described internationally (Hodgetts 2002) as authoritarian (i.e., a one-way downward flow of information and influence from leader to subordinates), paternalistic (i.e., a two-way interactional flow involving leader and subordinate pairs or dyads), and participative (i.e., two-way interactional flow involving leader and subordinates but also involving subordinate to subordinate information and influence flows). Most international research has focused on North American and European workers, and results show a preference for participative leadership styles. Younger managers are more likely to favor participative styles and company size has an impact too, with managers in smaller firms (e.g., 500 employees and less) showing more support for participative styles. However, paternalistic styles are preferred in Central and South America and in China (Aycan et al. 2000).

Haire, Ghiselli, and Porter (1966) found a preference for paternalistic styles of leadership in Japan, but that Japanese workers also favor the use of participation in the workplace more than many cultures. Japanese leaders have confidence in the ability of subordinates and rely on their subordinates to participate and show initiative. As stated earlier, Asian cultures tend to stress satisfaction with long-term job security and service to the collective valued more than in North American cultures and so the combination of paternalism and participation makes sense in Japan. However, at senior levels of management a basic difference between Japanese managers and American managers is obvious. The Japanese are taught to use variety amplification in problem solving, meaning that managers and their groups seek more information, pursue many alternatives, and have a long-term time orientation. To Americans, this seems like building in more uncertainty into the decision making. American executives, on the other hand, use variety reduction in problem solving, which limits the number of alternatives considered and reduces uncertainty. An American decision-making process is more likely to emphasize central problem aspects and to focus on attainable goals or objectives than would a process in Japan.

To summarize, one of the keys to leadership in international business settings is knowing what style and behaviors are best suited to the culture and adapting one's behavior accordingly (Trompenaars and Hampden-Turner 1998). In more emotionally expressive cultures, U.S. and European cultures for example, leaders avoid detached, cool, or ambiguous demeanors since these will be evaluated negatively. In more emotionally neutral cultures such as in Japan and China, leaders avoid warm or enthusiastic displays of feelings. Such emotional expressions in these cultures are interpreted as lacking in personal control and as being inconsistent with one's status as an authority.

Where Can Cultural Competence Be Developed?

Try taking an intellectual approach (Gudykunst, Hammer, and Wiseman 1977) to understanding another culture. Look for lectures, readings, films, and other multimedia presentations to gain an understanding of the target culture's people, customs, institutions, and values.

Try taking an area simulation approach (Gudykunst, Hammer, and Wiseman 1977) to understanding another culture. Volunteer for international meetings, either in-person or by videoconferencing, to create the environments or situations that are as similar as possible to working as an expatriate manager in that culture.

Recognize that a host country's culture neither can describe every individual who lives within that culture (e.g., think of all the variations within the U.S. culture and how different individual people living within our own culture can be) nor can a culture be described by a single individual representing it, that is, by a stereotype. To explore a new culture, create a notebook of stereotypes associated with that culture and in addition make entries in the notebook of examples of how much variation there is between individuals in that culture. Leave room for later comments as you learn to develop your thinking about the culture you are investigating.

It is a truism that talking about one's own culture is very difficult since we learn its elements when we are young, and they become as natural to us as breathing the air. With the goal of learning about one's own culture and how it is perceived by other cultures, volunteer to mentor or coach a member of your employer's organization that comes from a different culture of origin. Keep a diary of how your culture looks like through their eyes.

To avoid a closed-world perspective (Hofstede 2009), that is, a tendency to see any other culture's elements that are unknown or unclear as simply wrong or foolish, keep a lab-notes style notebook by noting any unknown cultural elements from any culture you are aware of and then note what investigating those elements reveals. Take a hypothesis testing approach to these investigations seeking to discover the underlying functions of cultural ideas that are unclear to you.

If you receive an expatriate assignment yourself, ask for cultural training, language instruction, and orientation or learning to provide familiarity with everyday matters in the host country (Mendenhall and Odou 1985). Specifically, you should ask for teachers to cover geography, climate, housing and schools, and attitudes/roles/customs of the host country (Shen 2005). Be aware that Shen (2005) estimates that the failure rate for U.S. managers going to other cultures at 30 to 85 percent but that Shen estimates European managers failing at expatriate assignments at only 5 to 10 percent.

CHAPTER 8

Socialization Competence

What Is Socialization Competence?

Organizational assimilation is the process by which individuals join, participate in, and leave an organization (Jablin 1987, 2001). Assimilation can be further divided into two parts: socialization and individualization. Socialization is a process by which an organization attempts to influence and change individuals to meet its needs (Kramer 2010). In contrast to socialization, individualization is the process by which individuals attempt to change organizations to meet the individual's needs. This idea of individualization can be characterized by changing small things, such as personalizing a workspace with pictures, to something much larger like negotiating a different work schedule. Some of the more obvious attempts at socialization occur when established members attempt to influence new members. Socialization and individualization are in constant tension with each other (Kramer 2010). Newcomers may enact individualization by demanding a certain work schedule as a condition for accepting a job and established members may object to giving up their established work schedules. Socialization attempts by other organizational members after being in a position for years (i.e., socialization of a well-established member by another long-time employee) may be illustrated by the trade-offs between role taking and role making (Katz and Kahn 1978). Role taking occurs when individuals adopt the role behaviors that are suggested by other organizational members, whereas role making occurs when individuals influence others to accept their concept of a role, in either case a type of personalization of the role.

Models of socialization have three phases (Kramer 2010). Prior to joining an organization, a potential employee is in the anticipatory socialization or prearrival phase. This is followed by a period of initial participation, which is experienced as a new member of an organization or employer. This phase is frequently called the encounter or entry phase. The third phase occurs as the individual worker has become an established or full organizational member. This period is known as the role management or role acquisition phase. A fourth time could be added, which would be disengagement or exit as it signifies when individuals leave the organization. The next sections consider each of these phases in turn.

The time prior to joining an organization is called anticipatory socialization. This time can further be divided into vocational anticipatory socialization, which is the process of selecting an occupation or career, and into organizational anticipatory socialization, which is the process of selecting an employing organization to join (Jablin 2001). Organizational anticipatory socialization generally occurs more quickly than vocational anticipatory socialization.

The encounter phase begins when an individual becomes an organizational member and assumes some organizational role with the new employer. Individuals experiencing dissonance between the employing organization's expectations and their own expectations developed during anticipatory socialization can be said to have encountered the reality of their new role (Louis 1980).

Role management, the third stage, involves the change from becoming a newcomer to becoming an established organizational member (Feldman 1976). Individuals become increasingly aware of the organization's culture as a control system and learn that as the culture adapts and changes over time the individual must adapt to any changes in the organizational culture. The final phase called exit can be divided into voluntary exit, where the individual initiates the change, and into involuntary exit, where others initiate the change (Bluedorn 1978).

An accepted explanation for organizational socialization is called uncertainty reduction theory (Berger and Bradac 1982). This theory states that individuals experience uncertainty about the lack of predictability in events on the job and they in turn seek out information to reduce that lack of predictability. The premise behind this search is that uncertainty is uncomfortable and so individuals seek out information to reduce their uncertainty and therefore reach a more comfortable state (Waldeck and Myers 2008). There are different types of uncertainty relevant to this theory; however, three types of uncertainty have been discussed (Berger and Bradac 1982). The first type is descriptive uncertainty, which is being unable to identify individuals (e.g., knowing who is responsible for what or who has supervisory authority); the second type is predictive uncertainty, which being unable to predict an individual's behavior in a given work situation (e.g., why an employee refuses or objects to project's deadline); and the third type is explanatory uncertainty, which is being unable to explain the reason for an individual's actions (e.g., why a supervisor issues a written reprimand for a refusal to meet a deadline versus responding by a verbal reprimand). Distinguishing between different types of uncertainty is important because it recognizes that individuals do not have to reduce all types of uncertainty in a situation to feel comfortable, that is, they can manage their uncertainty in a situation by reducing some types of uncertainty without needing to reduce all types of uncertainty.

To manage uncertainty, individuals often use cognitive responses rather than seeking out additional information (Kramer 2004). For example, by relying on past experiences, stereotypes, and imagined conversations, individuals can create their own information for use in dealing with their uncertainty-based discomfort. This might occur as an employee recalling a past situation as "In my last job when I refused a new assignment, that boss didn't react harshly to me so this will be okay too." A second means of managing uncertainty is the process of comparing various competing motives and comparing such motives as impression management with the social costs of seeking out new information, which may lead the newcomer to avoid seeking out the necessary information at all (e.g., "If I ask Sarah about how the boss will react, I may look foolish to her and I want to make sure that Sarah likes me"). Obviously, from this latter example, it is important to remember that cognitive work may lead the individual away from getting more accurate information about the new situation. This is perhaps more a function of the individual's level of social anxiety than it is a function of whether they are an introvert or an extravert by personality.

Sense making is an alternative theoretical explanation for socialization (Weick 1995). Unlike uncertainty management, sense making is concerned with how individuals understand or assign meaning to experiences and the achieved sense of meaning, rather than avoidance of discomfort, serves as the motive for the behavior. Generally, this involves retrospectively creating meaning to understand one's work experiences. For Weick, sense making is not an individual process, but rather an interactive, intersubjective process in which individuals create agreed-upon meanings for experiences through interpersonal communication. Sense making involves creating an identity and by making a commitment to particular interpretations, and individuals thereby create their identity. As individuals assign meaning to their past experience, they begin by recognizing their own work life identity and its relationship to the larger social context they are trying to understand. One example would be the employee who adopts a work identity as a committed employee to explain their long work hours. Another example might be the supervisor– mentor whose mentee fails and consequently quits their job. The supervisor might then conclude that the mentee was never qualified for the job and wouldn't have succeeded in any case. Thus, the supervisor maintains their own sense of competence.

Social exchange theory is a third theoretical explanation that is very applicable to the socialization process. In this theory, individuals can exchange money, goods, services, information, status, and even friendship for similar or dissimilar resources (Foa and Foa 1980). If the benefits of the exchange are equal or perhaps exceed the costs of the exchange, the individual is likely to continue the relationship. If on the other hand costs outweigh the benefits, individuals are likely to discontinue the relationship (Thibaut and Kelley 1959). A simple example might be the new employee who works longer hours than originally expected because they think their loyalty will lead to an early promotion. In addition to simple exchange ratios, this theory also considers how individuals compare their exchanges with others in similar roles before drawing conclusions about their own cost–benefit ratios. Each individual considered has a comparison level, meaning the person being socialized draws their own subjective judgment of the other person's cost–benefit ratio. Next the person being socialized is said to have a perception of their comparison level for alternatives, which means that such a person would also make judgments about what other roles they may adopt and what such roles may produce in terms of cost–benefit ratio. An example of the chain of judgments might be "My assignments are much less empowering than Sam's assignments are, but if I request a new assignment, I would have to start at the bottom again and that would be worse than what I have now." During anticipatory socialization, individuals collect cost–benefit information on alternative jobs and organizations, perhaps basing their job offer acceptance on these anticipated cost–benefit exchanges and comparison levels for alternatives. During the encounter phase, they learn how to function in their job and organization, all the while gathering exchange perceptions. They continue through to the later encounter phase as they evaluate the costs and benefits of continuing their occupation during further role management interactions. Finally, if at some point the exchange seems unacceptable, either compared to the expected ratio or in comparison to current alternatives, they leave their employment in that organization.

A fourth model for explaining socialization is social identity theory put forth by Ashforth and Mael (1989). According to this theory, individuals' self-concepts are composed of two types of identities. First are personal identities, which consist of various individual attributes, such as physical features, abilities, psychological characteristics, and vocational interests. Second are social identities based on perceptions of belonging to various groups, organizations, and societies. People tend to classify themselves and others in part due to associations with these social collectives. When they identify with the collective, they may personally feel that they identify with the successes and failures that the group has, but that does not mean that they have internalized all the values and attitudes of the group. They may also identify more with the subgroup, such as their own work group, and then with the larger organization. In addition, the identification is more likely to occur when the group's values and practices are distinct, the group is perceived as successful in important goal achievements, and out groups are readily identifiable and associated with failures, and individuals within the group identified with are judged to share important commonalities with other members.

As appealing as it may be separate out distinct personal and social identities, it is likely that the two interact and influence each other so that the distinction is somewhat artificial (Alvesson, Ashcraft, and Thomas 2008). Some personal characteristics such as race or occupation are also group identifiers, so it is difficult to distinguish between personal and social identity. Additionally, identity is not stagnant because individuals are simultaneously affiliated with multiple groups and organizations; they are constantly managing multiple identities (Cheney 1991). Managing multiple identities involves increasing and decreasing various associations over time. As a result, identity work is an ongoing process in which individuals attempt to achieve a coherent and a distinct identity. It is possible for individuals to strongly identify with an organization without being particularly committed to it, perhaps due to this potential commitment to multiple roles.

How Can Socialization Competence Be Assessed?

On an organizationwide basis, social characteristics of the workplace are captured well by corporate culture (Frost et al., 1991). The Corporate Culture Preference Scale is an assessment device that does not assess the current culture as it exists but instead allows the respondent to indicate their preference for an optimal or ideal culture (McShane and Von Glinow 2013). This is more assessment of the individual than of the situation, but it is clearly useful in orienting the reader toward future workplace situations.

Corporate Culture Preference Scale

Read each pair of statements in the Corporate Culture Preference Scale and circle the statement that describes the organization you would prefer to work for from each pair of statements. The scale does not attempt to measure your preference for every corporate culture—just a few of the more common varieties. Completing the scale a second time for your current situation can provide an indication of what is missing among your cultural preferences.

I WOULD PREFER TO WORK IN AN ORGANIZATION:

1a. Where employees work well together in teams.

-or-

1b. That produces highly respected products or services.

2a. Where top management maintains a sense of order in the workplace.

-or-

2b. Where the organization listens to customers and responds quickly to their needs.

3a. Where employees are treated fairly.

-or-

3b. Where employees continuously search for ways to work more efficiently.

4a. Where employees adapt quickly to new work requirements.

-or-

4b. Where corporate leaders work hard to keep employees happy.

5a. Where senior executives receive special benefits not available to other employees.

-or-

5b. Where employees are proud when the organization achieves its performance goals.

6a. Where employees who perform the best get paid the most.

-or-

6b. Where senior executives are respected.

7a. Where everyone gets her or his job done like clockwork.

-or-

7b. That is on top of innovations in the industry.

8a. Where employees receive assistance to overcome any personal problems.

-or-

8b. Where employees abide by company rules.

9a. That is always experimenting with new ideas in the marketplace.

-or-

9b. That expects everyone to put in 110 percent for peak performance.

10a. That quickly benefits from market opportunities.

-or-

10b. Where employees are always kept informed about what's happening in the organization.

11a. That can quickly respond to competitive threats.

-or-

11b. Where most decisions are made by the top executives.

12a. Where management keeps everything under control.

-or-

12b. Where employees care for each other.

Scoring

On each line below, write a 1 if you circled the statement and a 0 if you did not. Then add up the scores for each subscale.

Control Culture   ____ + ____ + ____ + ____ + ____ + ____ = ____
                        (2a)   (5a)   (6b)   (8b)   (11b) (12a)

Score interpretation: Low is 0, moderate is 1 to 2, and high is 3 to 6.

Performance Culture ____ + ____ + ____ + ____ + ____ + ____ = ____
                        (1b)   (3b)   (5b)   (6a)   (7a)   (9b)

Score interpretation: Low is 0 to 2, moderate is 3 to 4, and high is 5 to 6.

Relationship Culture ____ + ____ + ____ + ____ + ____ + ____ = ____
                        (1a)   (3a)   (4b)   (8a)   (10b) (12b)

Score interpretation: Low is 0 to 3, moderate is 4 t0 5, and high is 6.

Responsive Culture   ____ + ____ + ____ + ____ + ____ + ____ = ____
                        (2b)   (4a)   (7b)   (9a)   (10a) (11a)

Score Interpretation

Low is 0 to 3, moderate is 4 to 5, and high is 6.

Complete the scale a second time, but in this instance indicate what you think is most true of your current job and the organizational values in that context.

I WOULD DESCRIBE MY CURRENT ORGANIZATION'S CULTURE AS:

1a. Where employees work well together in teams.
                        -or-
1b. That produces highly respected products or services.

2a. Where top management maintains a sense of order in the workplace.

-or-

2b. Where the organization listens to customers and responds quickly to their needs.

3a. Where employees are treated fairly.

-or-

3b. Where employees continuously search for ways to work more efficiently.

4a. Where employees adapt quickly to new work requirements.

-or-

4b. Where corporate leaders work hard to keep employees happy.

5a. Where senior executives receive special benefits not available to other employees.

-or-

5b. Where employees are proud when the organization achieves its performance goals.

6a. Where employees who perform the best get paid the most.

-or-

6b. Where senior executives are respected.

7a. Where everyone gets her or his job done like clockwork.

-or-

7b. That is on top of innovations in the industry.

8a. Where employees receive assistance to overcome any personal problems.

-or-

8b. Where employees abide by company rules.

9a. That is always experimenting with new ideas in the marketplace.

-or-

9b. That expects everyone to put in 110 percent for peak performance.

10a. That quickly benefits from market opportunities.

-or-

10b. Where employees are always kept informed about what's happening in the organization.

11a. That can quickly respond to competitive threats.

-or-

11b. Where most decisions are made by the top executives.

12a. Where management keeps everything under control.

                        -or-

12b. Where employees care for each other.

Scoring

On each line below, write a 1 if you circled the statement and a 0 if you did not. Then add up the scores for each subscale.

Control Culture   _____ + _____ + _____ + _____ + _____ + _____ = _____

                (2a)   (5a)   (6b)   (8b)   (11b) (12a)

Score interpretation: Low is 0, moderate is 1 to 2, and high is 3 to 6.

Performance Culture _____ + _____ + _____ + _____ + _____ + _____ = _____

                (1b)   (3b)   (5b)   (6a)   (7a)   (9b)

Score interpretation: Low is 0 to 2, moderate is 3 to 4, and high is 5 to 6.

Relationship Culture _____ + _____ + _____ + _____ + _____ + _____ = _____

                (1a)   (3a)   (4b)   (8a) (10b) (12b)

Score Interpretation: Low is 0 to 3, moderate is 4 to 5, and high is 6.

Responsive Culture _____ + _____ + _____ + _____ + _____ + _____ = _____

                (2b)   (4a)   (7b)   (9a) (10a) (11a)

Score Interpretation

Low is 0 to 3, moderate is 4 to 5, and high is 6.

To compare your preferred culture scores with your current culture scores, use the following:

	Preferred – Current		
	Score	Score	Difference
Control culture	_____	– _____	= _____
Performance culture	_____	– _____	= _____

Relationship culture   _____ – _____ = _____

Responsive culture   _____ – _____ = _____

Control cultures value command and control principles of organization and place great legitimacy in their top executives. The values seek to align all work and employees and stress control and formalism.

Performance cultures value individual and organizational achievement. Here all events are measured against standards for effectiveness and efficiency. Competition and its rewards are stressed.

Relationship cultures are nurturing and promote individual well-being. Such an organization uses open communications systems, the right to fair treatment, an emphasis on cooperation and teamwork, and sharing to create organizational processes.

Responsive cultures strive to keep and practice openness to their corporate environment. These cultures make the competition about the entire organization and how it responds to opportunities in its environment.

Why Is Socialization Competence Important in Organizations?

During anticipatory socialization, individuals likely choose accept jobs in organizations based on the ease of identifying with the organization making the job offer, and conversely job hunters avoid other job offering organizations that they cannot identify with easily. Through a process of induction, training, and corporate education, the organizational representatives attempt to regulate employees' identities. As the newcomers learn about the organization's people and culture, they probably begin to identify more with the organization or subunit and begin to internalize its values and practices. If or when they cannot identify with the organization or view identifying with an alternative organization, they are likely consider leaving the organization.

Organizational anticipatory socialization involves two main activities. The first part of the socialization process involves an organization providing information to attract or recruit potential members. The individuals seeking information as part of their efforts to find organizations to join are involved in reconnaissance. The second part of the anticipatory socialization process is the actual selection process in which individuals and organizational representatives are involved in job interviews, during which decisions are made about whether individuals will join the organization. A third part of the process will also be briefly discussed later, but there are in total three pre-entry phases. Research suggests that organizations improve their recruitment by focusing on recruitment objectives, recruitment strategies, and recruitment activities. One consequence of the aforementioned is that organizations today tend to release large amounts of public information about themselves in pursuit of recruitment successes.

The recruitment and reconnaissance processes do not always work equally well for all applicants. People from different ethnic, economic, or social groups may not have equal access to relevant information, such as campus recruiters. Networking may be particularly problematic for many individuals, resulting in current employees filtering out diverse and unique individuals in their referrals. Limited access constrains opportunities for applicants, but it also prevents the organization from gaining valuable and possibly unique perspectives of the missed recruits. Screening job interviews are frequently viewed as a process for reducing the number of individuals consider for hire, but they help in determining person-to-job fit as well. Research focused on evaluating person-to-organization fit finds that achieving a good person-to-organization fit can be more important than selecting for the best job skills, particularly in cases where much of the work is learned on the job. Research on job interviewing is disheartening. Applicants might expect to speak more of the time than their interviewers do during interviews, but research consistently shows that interviewers tend to dominate the conversation, speaking as much as 60 to 80 percent of the time. In addition, interviewers typically make their decisions about whether the applicant should continue to the next level during the first five minutes of the interview, and yet the interviewers tend to talk most of the time and ask closed-ended questions that provide applicants little opportunity to speak and create an impression. Interviewers also tend to weigh negative information, especially if it is revealed early in the conversation, more heavily than positive information. This is most likely relating to the fact that many interviewers are looking for reasons to reject candidates early in the process due to frequent overabundance of applicant files. Far less research examines second or on-site interviews, but in addition to being the time when organizations make job offer decisions, the second interview differs from screening interviews in at least four important ways. Second interviews typically occur on-site while the organization is conducting big business and thus have a stronger impact on anticipatory socialization. Second, on-site interviews tend to involve sessions lasting anywhere from a few hours to more than a day, particularly for its higher-level management positions. Screening interviews typically involve two individuals having a conversation, while second interviews frequently involve multiple interviewers and, in some cases, even multiple applicants. Finally, screening interviews have rather predictable formats with many being characterized by the use of standardized questions and second interviews are much more fluid in their structure. Given these characteristics, second interviews offer a better opportunity for complete information exchange. An unfortunate result of screening interviews is that both the interviewer and interviewee are involved in self-presentation and impression management during the interview and they tend to give limited focus to obtaining accurate or realistic information on which to make their decisions; if are you the applicant the decision on whether to join the organization and if you are the recruiter on whether to offer a position the applicant. Applicants and organizational representatives can pass on inaccurate information out of self-interest (e.g., the applicant may be too focused on winning the job offer and fail to seek out an accurate picture of the job or the organization's culture). As a result, individuals may enter the workplace with very high expectations that may not be met. Organizations likewise may have unrealistic expectations of new employees and may spend the interview conveying overly positive impressions of the job and the employing organization. Many studies have indicated the impact of unmet expectations is dissatisfaction and turnover in newcomers (Wanous 1992). The current recruitment process probably propagates this problem since organizations are concerned with attracting the best applicants, as well as applicants who are eager for job offers, and in the process achieve many poor person-to-organization outcomes. In the end, applicants often search for realistic information on their own. Those applicants with network contacts probably have an advantage here.

Socialization strategies can be described in a variety of terms. One distinction is between group versus individual socialization. In group socialization, a collection of newcomers is put through the same orientation and training simultaneously. In contrast, individual socialization involves assimilation through an individual orientation or training. A second distinction is formal versus informal training. In formal training, the newcomers are separated from co-workers and placed with a trainer to learn a particular skill or procedure before moving into the actual workplace. Informal training is essentially on-the-job training in which newcomers begin performing their jobs immediately. A third distinction is sequential versus random socialization. This has to do with the order in which new tasks are learned. In a sequential socialization strategy, newcomers learn their tasks in a specified order. In some cases, they may not be allowed to move on to the next skill until having mastered the previous skill. In random socialization, the newcomer learns skills as they randomly appear in the work, and so is often associated with informal, on-the-job training. The fourth distinction is fixed versus variable, which deals with the amount of time allowed on learning each skill: In fixed socialization, newcomers know exactly how much time will be spent on various activities, whereas in variable socialization the amount of time for each learning of a skill is unspecified. Another distinction is serial versus disjunctive socialization. When a newcomer experiences tasks in the role as they are assigned to be completed while an experienced individual serves as the newcomer's temporary role model or mentor. In disjunctive socialization, no one is assigned to the newcomer to help their learning of the new role. Although this could be due to lack of management concern, often it is because the person who previously served in the role has left the organization or because the position is newly created and so there is no one who knows exactly how to perform the job. A final distinction is divestiture versus investiture socialization. In divestiture processes, the organization attempts to strip away the unique and individual characteristics of a newcomer and replace them with standard characteristics of that the organization desires for its members. An obvious example is military boot camp. In investiture socialization, the organization appreciates individual's uniqueness and comes to reaffirm it and build upon it with the intent of convey a message that it values the newcomer's unique talents and perspectives.

Socialization of employees is a principal means by which organizations maintain or manage their corporate culture. It is the blending of formal and informal control systems that makes corporate culture a valuable part of strategic management and really all corporate operations. The more quickly and effectively an employee is socialized, the sooner that employee becomes a productive worker within the organization. The functions of socialization include providing a sense of identity to members of the organization as well as an easily applied code for interpreting the meaning of significant events with the corporation. Socialization furthers and supports the behavioral controls of the corporation and reinforces the values of the organization. The targets of socialization in most organizations fits with the previous conclusions about the functions of socialization. Socialization as a learning process about the history of the corporation's traditions, myths, and rituals as well as learning about the language unique to the corporation (e.g., common acronyms, slang, and jargon) give a sense of identity. Socialization also speaks to the ways that proficiency in performance must be demonstrated, both in the sense of task performance and in the sense of social performance of work roles and these together teach the newcomer the behavioral control systems. Adopting as one's own the spoken and unspoken goals and values of the corporation along with information on formal and informal power relations within the corporation teach the newcomer how to interpret the meaning of events and statements made by others. In a sense then, socialization supports and promotes the organization's culture, which itself functions to further efficiency and effectiveness in the organization.

Moving past the idea of socialization at the newcomer stage allows us to question how the impact of socialization matters to managers throughout their careers in the organization. Four ongoing impacts will be described here: Corporate cultures that are strong versus weak matter to the managers in that corporation, and how employees fit into the corporate culture matters in terms of the performance or even decision to leave the corporation, or how adaptive or agile the corporate culture is matters and therefore socialization into a culture affects employees' resistance to change and that too matters.

A strong corporate culture is the one in which a consensus exists regarding the nature of that culture, and it is a culture possessing an intensity that is recognizable to outsiders. High consensus exists when all employees agree on organizational goals and values. High intensity in the cultural expressions is demonstrated when all employee behaviors are consistent with cultural expectations. It is obvious, for example, that Microsoft has a strong culture typified by competitive success in the software industry and typified by their employees accepting high workloads and work schedule demands on its employees. But that observation also points toward that fact that strong corporate cultures often occur in organizations that outperform their rivals. Such organizations have greater degrees of goal alignment throughout their various units, their employees show high levels of work motivation, and behavioral controls seem to operate without excessive bureaucratic controls that are formal and standardized.

There are disadvantages to cultural strength that every manager should be aware of as they progress through their careers. Strong cultures make merging with another organization difficult and can affect the success of corporate acquisitions. Over conformity to a strong culture can be prevent creativity and corporate entrepreneurship from developing when needed and may reach down even to the level of group decision making when conformity is too extreme. Most corporate environments are seeing increasingly faster and greater changes and whether these changes are based on regulatory or economic changes, or just from new competitive initiatives from corporate rivals, strong cultures can be restrictive and make changes harder. Overly strong cultures are probably not the best for organizational performance in the long run.

Managers should be concerned about the existence of subcultures within their organization's culture and whether these subcultures arise from different units operating with independence or because of strong leaders within the corporation promoting different norms and values within their own areas, with a net result that subcultures weaken cultural strength. Of course, the extreme of this would be when countercultures are created with values that do not match those of the rest of organization. Countercultures may only temporarily limit corporate performance, however, since a counterculture may represent an innovative solution to environmental changes and therefore be necessary evolution in the culture.

A second way that socialization matters is that this social learning process is one element in the person–organization fit scheme. This fit, or the degree to which an individual employee's personality and values match well with the corporate culture, can predict the person's overall job satisfaction, but it may also predict levels of job stress and trust in supervision or co-workers. Corporate cultures have been said to pursue becoming strong cultures in order to attract the best new employees, such that even before job interviews job applicants can select only firms with expressed values that match their own. Once past the interview stage, selection processes in a strong culture are likely to include the potential hire's fit with the values and goals of the corporation's culture. Not to be minimized, however, is the process of attrition as an example of person–organization fit. Employees may quit or be terminated after a period of employment when their values and goals conflict with the organization's goals and values. Thus, in the attraction–selection–attrition (ASA) framework, those individuals who don't "fit" will be unhappy and/or ineffective when working within the corporate culture.

Organizations use socialization as a form of cultural communication, especially in the sense of communicating about the organization's desired culture. In a sense then, socialization is a necessary form of cultural communication and early in the employee's tenure in the company they learn important messages about the underlying values of the organization as well as its explicit goals. But socialization can also be seen as an ongoing process where learning in formal training, learning by observing what behavior gets rewarded and punished, and the impact of exposure to role models are all forms of socialization and organizational communication. For example, employees see how corporate leaders behave, what those leaders pay attention to, how those leaders allocate rewards, how they hire and fire individuals, and of course how leaders react to crises. Public events celebrating corporate successes can be viewed as socialization processes in this regard.

Changing an organization's culture is feasible but difficult. It may occur by necessity when there are changes in leadership since new leaders bring their own goals and values into the organization and that is clear signal for organizational change. Mergers and acquisitions can also signal cultural change as the need for two organizations coming together requires either one prior existing culture to change to match the other's culture or it may require a new, third corporate culture being created. These changes are challenging since the cultural elements are usually deeply ingrained and the behavioral norms and rewards are well learned. Some experts hold that the assumptions about what leads to corporate success are often unconsciously held and practiced and that these deepest elements of culture must be unlearned and changed too (Schein 2004).

In terms of the impact of socialization on an organization's current employees, a major topic capable of attracting all managers' attention is overcoming resistance to change. The resistance to change can be based on fear (e.g., fear of failure, of loss, of the unknown), it can be based on anxiety about the disruption in interpersonal relationships that may exist under the status quo, or in some cases change may be seen as a political threat to those who hold such power, and when strong cultures exist even the current corporate culture can lead to the resistance to change. There are four types of behavioral responses to organizational change. First is disengagement, which implies a sort of psychological withdrawal from tasks or activities associated with change. In response, managers can confront employees about their withdrawal and seek to draw them out as active responders. Second is disidentification, which reflects the employee's feelings that their work identity may be threatened by the proposed change. Managers can encourage employees who disidentify to explore their feelings with the manager and to seek to transmit more positive feelings about the changes to the employee. Disenchantment is another type of response that is described by workers openly voicing anger toward requested changes. Managers can deal with disenchantment by allowing the employee to vent so that the employee can come to terms with their anger publicly. The final type of response is disorientation and is typified by employees who voice feelings of loss and confusion due to the proposed changes. Managers can explain to such an employee that change does relate to the organization's vision and seek to clarify any implications that may be confusing to the employee. To summarize, managers can use communication skills to deal with employees' disengagement and disorientation, and when mitigating employee's disidentification and disenchantment, the manager can use empathy and support (i.e., emotional intelligence-based skills).

Another approach to resistance to change that has strong practical implications is Lewin's force field change model. This approach asks the manager to look at the factors supporting change simultaneously with the factors opposing change (i.e., supporting the status quo). The manager is asked to find points of leverage among the factors such that either factors supporting change can be strengthened or factors opposing change can be weakened. Take for example, employees asked to move from a status quo system for scheduling meetings by mass e-mails to all meeting participants versus scheduling meetings using accessible software for calendars (e.g., Outlook's calendar function). The goal of faster, more efficient scheduling for meetings is a factor strongly supporting such a change and the fear of learning a new set of software commands is a factor that will lead to resistance to the proposed change (see Figure 8.1 for more

Factors Supporting a Change to an Accessible, Software-based Calendar	Factors Supporting the Status Quo of Using Mass Emails to Schedule Meetings
Faster and more efficient scheduling	Need to learn unknown software
Less absenteeism due to omissions or forgetting of agreed to times	Must allow others access to own existing calendar
Reminders are automatic	Must have approved rationale for times blocked-out as unavailable
Hard limits for beginning and ending times	More difficult to avoid meetings and group assignments

Figure 8.1 *Scheduling meetings as an example of Lewin's change model*

examples). In Lewin's theory, the term unfreezing is used to indicate how the manager will remove rewards for current behavior and refreezing is the term used to implement or use existing rewards that will support the proposed changes. It is this latter point, the need to use either the formal reward system or to rely on organization's culture to support the change, that really must be thought through and implemented by the manager seeking to overcome resistance to change. Without it, any changes made may only be temporary.

Where Can Socialization Competence Be Developed?

An obvious means to gain socialization competence is to ask to be assigned new employees to socialize. This will allow you practice your presentation and mentoring skills but it will also help you develop appreciation for the perspectives held by newcomers.

If you have been in your current position for two years or more, ask your Human Resources Department to see their materials for onboarding of new employees. Review these and compare with your observations of your workgroup or your peers. Going further after that you can ask your Human Resources Department for exit interview summaries from interactions with employees who recently quit.

You can volunteer to serve as a mentor if your organization has a formal mentorship program and if your organization does not have such a program look for someone to approach as an informal mentor.

If you have a mentor yourself, share your observations with that person.

CHAPTER 9

Health Competence

What Is Health Competence?

It is clear that in the modern world adults of working age are concerned about health issues. One look at the Internet these days will produce such headlines as:

- Obesity is an epidemic.
- Mortality rates increase for middle-age males.
- Government fails to protect citizens against lead poisoning in their water.
- Dementia threatens the Baby Boom Generation.
- Adults fail to get enough sleep.

A recent survey reported that one or more major stressors affect 77 percent of Americans at work, such as a long commute to get to work, high demands on the job, and the risk of being fired or laid off. In a second survey of 115,000 employees from 33 countries, respondents in Japan reported the most stress-related health complaints followed by Canada, Ukraine, Finland, Hong Kong, and Hungary (Lester 2006). Surveys conducted by the World Families and Work Institute show that 44 percent of Americans say they are overworked, up from 28 percent who felt this way a few years earlier. Almost 25 percent of Canadian employees work more than 50 hours per week, compared with only 10 percent a decade ago. More recently, Canadians identified work overload is the second-highest stressor, after insufficient salary. In another study, 40 percent of Americans say they have not had a real vacation within the previous two years wherein vacations consist of leisure travel for a week or more to a destination at least 100 miles from home (Galinsky 2005).

It is clear too that the strategic advantages to corporations of a safe and healthy workforce have been documented. Safe and healthy workplaces (1) show higher productivity due to workers losing fewer work days due to sickness or injury, (2) show increased efficiency and higher work quality, (3) demonstrate lower medical and insurance costs, (4) show evidence of reduced workers' compensation rates and even fewer direct payments because of fewer workers' compensation claims being filed, and (5) improved industry and community reputations as an employer of choice for future employees (Jackson, Schuler, and Werner 2016). However, what are the benefits of increased awareness of well-being and workplace health practices to the individual manager? While it is true that the concerns of work adjustment and well-being go far beyond traditional Occupational Safety and Health Administration (OSHA) topics on freedom from injury and illness at work, a good place to gain a more complete understanding of work adjustment and well-being would be to examine individuals' stress perceptions and responses.

Stress is an adaptive response to a situation that is perceived as either challenging or threatening to the individual's well-being. If we are to look at a person in a job context, then examples of stress are going to be things like a new task, a new job assignment, working with the new co-worker, being supervised by a new boss, time limits, or work in hot and noisy environments. Stress can be defined as both a physiological condition as well as a psychological condition. In both cases, stress prepares us to adapt to the environmental conditions of either challenge or potentially hostile or noxious conditions. In the job context, this might mean the kind of adrenaline and hyper-alert state that we feel when we must do a presentation, or speaking before a large group of people, or try a new activity or task for the first time. It is both the psychological perception of feeling nervous and the physiological responses of feeling your heart beat faster or feeling your face flush.

Psychologists make a fundamental distinction between what is called stress and distress. Working under stress is a notion that sometimes people work better when they have an audience or when they have a moderate degree of challenge. For example, the notion of social facilitation is often responsible for athletes performing at a record level when in a a significant competition in front of a large audience as opposed to the kinds of results they see when they are practicing or working out in private. Another example of stress might be individuals who say they do their best work when they are facing a deadline. Distress, as opposed to stress, is a concept that indicates that the stress is dysfunctional, and stress interferes with performance of the job, the task, or the interaction.

What Causes Job Stress?

Stress is the unconscious preparation to react to a demand. It is a genuine psychological response in that sense. The stressor is the person, the event, or the task that triggers the stress response. Everyday stressors on the job could be caused by tasks or activities, by people, or by challenging situations, but in all cases they are external situational events. Distress, which is sometimes called strain since it is the adverse psychological, physical, behavioral, and organizational consequences that may occur as a result of stressful events, is our primary concern in job stress.

Going back now and looking at stress sources, we can see some basic categories for job stressors. First, hindrance stressors are demands that are perceived as hindering progress toward personal accomplishments or goal attainment. Hindrance stressors tend to trigger negative emotions such as anger and anxiety. Second, job challenge stressors on the job are stressful demands that are perceived as opportunities for learning, growth, and achievement. Challenge stressors then are events on the job that trigger positive emotions; examples would be pride or enthusiasm on the job. Role conflict, one of the best examples of a hindrance stressor, refers to a situation in which there are conflicting expectations that other people hold about a job and its tasks. As an example, think of the kinds of role conflict that a call center operator might experience. In this example, the person may have expectations to be courteous and socially responsive to the caller. At the same time, they must be analytical, receptive, and sensitive to the questions and demands that the caller is making. Finally, the operator may be trying to meet the role expectations of the boss or the company regarding how to correctly apply company policy. As we can see in this example, there may be times when all three of these can be satisfied and times when all three of these types of role expectations can be impossible to satisfy or comply with would be the situation to represent job stress best.

Another type of hindrance stress on the job would be role ambiguity. Role ambiguity refers to the lack of information regarding what is required of a role, as well as the unpredictability regarding the consequences of performance in that role. An example of this would be new employees in their first week on the job. New employees are often concerned about what they should do and when they should do it. Later, an employee may be clear on what the tasks are, yet concerned about how their performance in that job will be evaluated. That ambiguity over an evaluation can be stressful and is an excellent example of role ambiguity. A third example of role stress that helps us understand hindrance stress would be role overload. Role overload occurs when the number of demanding roles a person holds is so high that the person cannot perform all the roles that they receive from others. In other words, having more to do than the employee has time in which to accomplish different tasks or activities. Finally, a fourth example of job stress has been defined as daily hassles. The concept of daily hassles reflects the relatively minor day-to-day demands on the job that might get in the way of accomplishing the things that are more important or having higher priority. These hassles then are interfering with our hoped-for act performance of the higher priority tasks. So, e-mail would be a great example of that in many employee's jobs today. Managers often report having 100 to 200 e-mails to respond to every day, many of which are of minor importance or even irrelevant and represent daily hassles.

Working hours would be an example of yet another stressor. Why do employees work long hours? One explanation is the combined effects of technology and globalization. One executive states that everyone in this industry is working harder now, because of e-mail, wireless access, and globalization. A second factor is that many people are caught up in consumerism. They want to buy more goods and services; doing so requires more income through more extended hours. A third reason, which we might call the ideal worker norm, is that the professional expects themselves and others to work more extended hours. It should be pointed out that strong evidence exists for immediate and long-term effects of work–family conflicts as those conflicts impact employee well-being (Grant-Vallone and

Donaldson 2001). This directly included in the assessments in this chapter simply due to space constraints.

Job stress may also be described as an adaptive response to a situation and perceived as challenging or threatening to a person's well-being (Quick 1997). Stress prepares us to adapt to hostile or aversive environmental conditions. For example, our heart rate increases, muscles tighten, breathing speeds up, and perspiration increases. Our body also moves more blood to the brain, releases adrenaline and other hormones, fuels the system by releasing glucose and fatty acids, activates systems that sharpen the senses, and conserves resources by shutting down our immune system. In short, stress is a negative evaluation of the external environment and its potential. In this sense, it would be fair to say that stress responses occur before even conscious reactions do (Lazarus 2006).

Job stress is typically described as a negative experience; this is known as distress. The distress is the degree of physiological, psychological, and behavioral deviation from healthy functioning—some stress, however, can have positive qualities and arise from the idea that part of life is activating and motivating when people confront opportunities to achieve new goals, change their environment, and succeed in life's challenges. However, turning toward distress and its toll on the human body, many people report tension headaches, muscle pain, and related health problems due to the stress response. Other complaints might include cardiovascular diseases, such as heart attacks and strokes, or even moodiness and depression, causing a lack of satisfaction and reduced organizational commitment.

Before identifying the ways in which individuals vary in their response to stressors, we must first understand extreme or unlawful causes of job stress. The causes of job stress we have referred to as stressors should include any condition that places a physical or emotional demand on a worker. But sometimes job stress is abnormal and even illegal. For example, psychological harassment is an example of a job stressor (Pearson and Porath 2005). Psychological harassment includes repeated hostile or unwanted contact, verbal statements, actions, and gestures that undermine an employee's dignity or psychological or physical integrity. This definition covers a broad landscape of behaviors from threats and bullying to subtle yet persistent forms of incivility. Sexual harassment is a type of harassment in which a person's employment or job performance is conditional. It depends on unwanted sexual relations, called a quid pro quo harassment. In this situation, a person experiences sexual conduct from others that unreasonably interferes with their work performance and creates an intimidating, hostile, or offensive work environment.

Differences Between People in How They Experience Stressors

Individuals experience different stress levels when exposed to the same stressor. One factor is the employee's physical health. Regular exercise and a healthy lifestyle produce a larger store of energy to cope with stress. The second individual difference is the coping strategies employees used to ward off stressors. People sometimes figure out ways to remove the stressor or minimize its presence. Other coping mechanisms include seeking support from others, reframing the stressor in a more positive light, and blaming others for the stressor, and denying the existence of stressors. Some coping strategies work better for specific stressors, and some work well for all stressors. Some people tend to rely on one or two coping strategies, and those who rely on generally poor coping strategies, such as denying the stressor exists, are going to experience more stress overall. Thus, someone who uses a less effective coping mechanism in a situation would experience more stress in response to that situation. Personality is the third and possibly most important reason people experience different levels of stress when faced with the same stressor (Nelson and Sutton 1990). Individuals with low neuroticism and high emotional stability usually experience lower stress levels because they are less prone to anxiety, depression, and other negative emotions. Extroverts also tend to experience lower stress. People with a positive self-concept, including high self-esteem, self-efficacy, and internal locus of control, feel more confident and in control when faced with a stressor. In other words, they tend to have a stronger sense of optimism. To summarize the influences of stress perceptions and their consequences, Figure 9.1 presents a model for how work stress happens to the individual worker.

How Can Health Competence Be Assessed?

The Job Stress Survey (Spielberger and Reheiser 1994) is designed to measure stress factors for most workers across a wide variety of positions and

Environmental Factors	Organizational Factors	Personal Factors
-Unsafe environments	-Task Demands	-Family Problems
-Job Insecurity	-Role Demands	-Financial Worries
-Technological Change	-Interpersonal Conflicts	-Personality Tendencies

Potential Stressors

Individual Differences in:
-Perceptions
-Job Experience
-Social Support
-Self-efficacy
-Health Status

Experienced
Job Stress

Physical Symptoms	Psychological Symptoms	Behavioral Symptoms
*Headaches	*Anxiety	*Productivity
*High Blood Pressure	*Depression	*Turnover
*Heart Disease	*Reduced Job Satisfaction	*Addiction

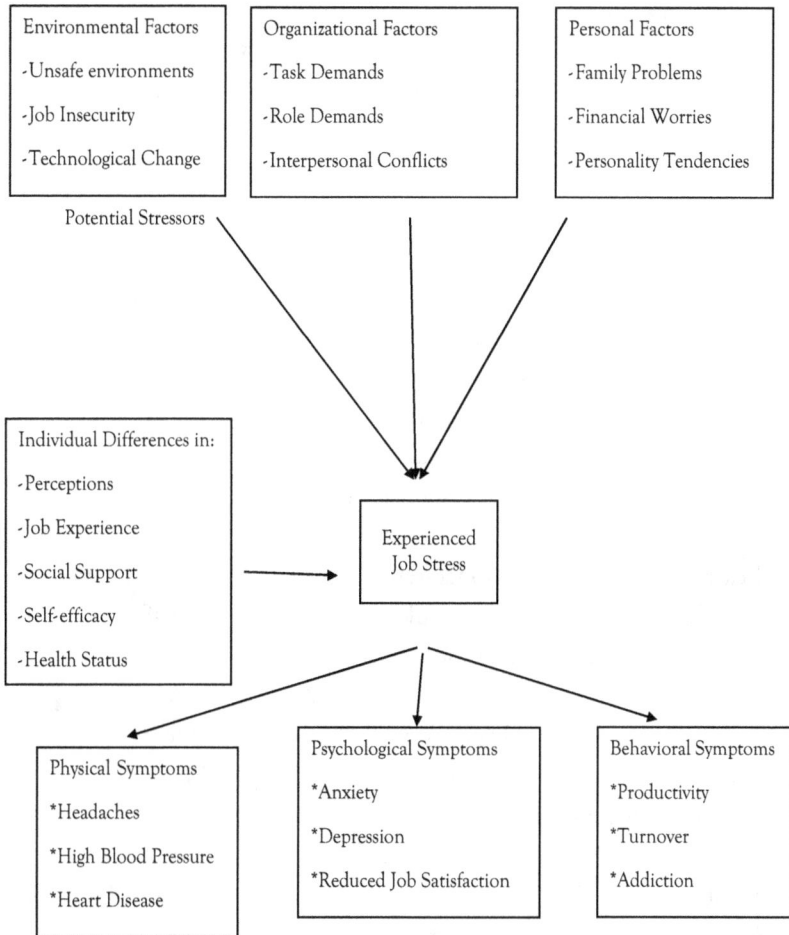

Figure 9.1 How the individual experiences job stress

organizations. It attempts to assess factors that could be called generic stressors, which might be present in any job. Rather than focusing on the frequency of a factor's occurrence, this scale asks the individual to directly respond to how stress-inducing the factor is for the worker.

Job Stress Survey Form

Rate each of the following situations as to how much job stress it causes you to perceive.

1. Assignment of new duties.

| 1 | 2 | 3 | 4 | 5 | 6 | 7 | 8 | 9 |

Least   Moderately   Most
Stressful   Stressful   Stressful

2. Dealing with crisis situations.

| 1 | 2 | 3 | 4 | 5 | 6 | 7 | 8 | 9 |

Least   Moderately   Most
Stressful   Stressful   Stressful

3. Performing tasks not in your job description.

| 1 | 2 | 3 | 4 | 5 | 6 | 7 | 8 | 9 |

Least   Moderately   Most
Stressful   Stressful   Stressful

4. Being assigned increased responsibility.

| 1 | 2 | 3 | 4 | 5 | 6 | 7 | 8 | 9 |

Least   Moderately   Most
Stressful   Stressful   Stressful

5. Critical on-the-spot decisions.

| 1 | 2 | 3 | 4 | 5 | 6 | 7 | 8 | 9 |

Least   Moderately   Most
Stressful   Stressful   Stressful

6. Frequent interruptions.

| 1 | 2 | 3 | 4 | 5 | 6 | 7 | 8 | 9 |

Least   Moderately   Most
Stressful   Stressful   Stressful

7. Frequent change, boring to demanding.

| 1 | 2 | 3 | 4 | 5 | 6 | 7 | 8 | 9 |

Least   Moderately   Most
Stressful   Stressful   Stressful

8. Excessive paperwork.

| 1 | 2 | 3 | 4 | 5 | 6 | 7 | 8 | 9 |

Least   Moderately   Most
Stressful   Stressful   Stressful

9. Meeting deadlines.

| 1 | 2 | 3 | 4 | 5 | 6 | 7 | 8 | 9 |

Least   Moderately   Most
Stressful   Stressful   Stressful

10. Insufficient personal time.

1	2	3	4	5	6	7	8	9
Least				Moderately				Most
Stressful				Stressful				Stressful

11. Lack of opportunity for advancement.

1	2	3	4	5	6	7	8	9
Least				Moderately				Most
Stressful				Stressful				Stressful

12. Fellow workers not doing their jobs.

1	2	3	4	5	6	7	8	9
Least				Moderately				Most
Stressful				Stressful				Stressful

13. Inadequate support by your supervisor.

1	2	3	4	5	6	7	8	9
Least				Moderately				Most
Stressful				Stressful				Stressful

14. Lack of recognition for your good work.

1	2	3	4	5	6	7	8	9
Least				Moderately				Most
Stressful				Stressful				Stressful

15. Inadequate or poor-quality equipment.

1	2	3	4	5	6	7	8	9
Least				Moderately				Most
Stressful				Stressful				Stressful

16. Difficulty getting along with your supervisor.

1	2	3	4	5	6	7	8	9
Least				Moderately				Most
Stressful				Stressful				Stressful

17. Negative attitudes toward the organization.

1	2	3	4	5	6	7	8	9
Least				Moderately				Most
Stressful				Stressful				Stressful

18. Not participating in decisions.

1	2	3	4	5	6	7	8	9
Least				Moderately				Most
Stressful				Stressful				Stressful

19. Poor or inadequate supervision.

1	2	3	4	5	6	7	8	9
Least				Moderately				Most
Stressful				Stressful				Stressful

20. Poorly motivated co-workers.

1	2	3	4	5	6	7	8	9
Least				Moderately				Most
Stressful				Stressful				Stressful

Scoring

Job Pressure Score = Sum items 1 to 10.

Low scores are between 10 and 30, moderate scores 31 to 69, high scores range from 70 to 90.

Lack of Organizational Support Score = Sum items 11 to 20.

Low scores are between 10 and 30, moderate scores 31 to 69, high scores range from 70 to 90

Several physical symptom inventories exist (Spector, 1988; Tuerluin et al., 2016; Wahler, 1968), which ask for a self-report of symptoms related to stress levels. These are usually in a yes/no response format and cover recent (i.e., within the last week) experiences. What follows is a representative sample of symptoms for your use created for this book.

Self-Report Form for Job Stress Symptoms

Put an "X" in the box under the answer that is appropriate.

	No	Sometimes
1. Dizziness	☐	☐
2. Muscle pain	☐	☐
3. Fainting	☐	☐
4. Neck pain	☐	☐
5. Back pain	☐	☐
6. Excessive sweating	☐	☐

7. Lack of energy ☐ ☐

8. Headache ☐ ☐

9. Blurred vision ☐ ☐

10. Bloated feeling in the abdomen ☐ ☐

11. Nausea or upset stomach ☐ ☐

12. Shortness of breath ☐ ☐

13. Tingling in the fingers ☐ ☐

14. Pressure or tight feeling in the chest ☐ ☐

15. Trembling when with other people ☐ ☐

16. Sudden fright for no reason ☐ ☐

17. Worry ☐ ☐

18. Disturbed sleep ☐ ☐

19. Feeling down or depressed ☐ ☐

20. Anxiety or panic attacks ☐ ☐

Scoring

No = 0   Sometimes = 1

A sum score of 10 or more indicates a high level of psychosomatic complaints.

Why Is Health Competence Important in Organizations?

Individual Mechanisms for Coping With Stress

It is clear that an individual's characteristics influences their stress coping process (Nelson and Sutton 1990). For example, many people deny the existence of their stress and endure more severe outcomes. This avoidance strategy creates a vicious cycle, because of failure, stress becomes another stressor on top of the one that created distress in the first place. Preventing this vicious cycle, employers and employees need to apply one or more of the following stress management strategies: remove the stressor, withdraw from the stressor, change stress perceptions, control stress consequences, and seek out social support.

Withdrawing from the presence of the stressor is another coping mechanism. Removing a stressor may be an ideal solution. At times this is not possible, and an alternative strategy is needed. Permanent withdrawal occurs when employees are transferred to jobs that better fit their competencies and values, whereas withdrawing temporarily from stressors is the most common or frequent way in which workers manage stress. Vacations and holidays, for example, provide essential means by which workers can recover from the stress of their everyday work lives to re-energize. Many firms also provide innovative ways for employees to withdraw from stressful work throughout the day such as game rooms, cafeteria areas, or even exercise facilities.

A reduction in experienced stress levels can also be achieved by altering one's stress perceptions such that positive self-evaluations and an optimistic outlook is emphasized. Personal goal setting and behavior modification plans can reduce the stress that people experience when they enter work settings. Research has also suggested that some forms of humor can improve optimism and create positive emotions. A healthy lifestyle is an effective stress management strategy because it controls stressors' consequences and one means to this end is engaging in regular exercise. Research indicates that physical exercise reduces the physiological consequence of stress by helping employees moderate their breathing, heart rate, muscle tension, and stomach acidity. Many companies offer yoga, Pilates, meditation, and other programs throughout the workday.

Research indicates that various forms of meditation reduce anxiety, reduce blood pressure, muscle tension, and has a positive effect on heart rate. Wellness programs can also help control the consequences of stress. These programs inform employees about better nutrition and fitness, regular sleep patterns, and other healthy habits. Many large employers offer employee assistance programs (EAPs). EAPs may include counseling and services that help employees resolve marital, financial, and work-related issues. EAP counseling varies with industries. Social support is yet another resource employee can tap into for support.

Social support occurs when co-workers, supervisors, family members, friends, and others provide emotional and informational support to buffer and individual's stressful experience. For instance, one recent study found that employee's managers were good sources of social support and employee's with such managers experienced fewer stress symptoms than did employees whose managers were less empathetic. This social support potentially improves a person's optimism and self-confidence, because support makes people feel valued and worthy. Some social support sources provide information, so healthy persons can interpret, comprehend, and remove the stressor based on the advice provided by the information source. For instance, to reduce new employee stress, co-workers could describe ways to handle demanding customers.

One approach to coping with stress called the transactional theory of stress holds that an individual appraises their responses to the stressor in both cognitive and behavioral terms. What should I feel? And what can I do? These are the types of questions this theory sees as the foundation of coping. Coping refers to both the behaviors and thoughts people use to manage both stressful demands they face, and the emotions associated with those stressful demands (Folkman et al. 1986). In this transactional approach, we split up coping strategies as behavioral versus cognitive. Behavioral coping involves a set of physical activities that are used to deal with a stressful situation. Liptak and Leutenberg (2006) posit, for example, a person with deadlines might choose to cope by working faster or longer. In contrast to such behavioral coping, cognitive coping refers to the thoughts that are involved in trying to deal with this stressful situation. For example, when faced with the same deadline as a peer, a second individual might respond by thinking about strategies for managing time to complete all the required tasks and duties. This response is more of a plan, or a judgment, that it is a set of behaviors or actions.

While the type of coping method chosen has just been described, what remains is the object of the coping with the two options, referred to as the focus. Problem-focused coping refers to behaviors and cognitions intended to manage the stressful situation itself as the object of coping.

Using the second example of deadline pressure, that person thought of a strategy for coping with the time pressures more efficiently. Here the person is expected to respond directly to the problem of time pressure rather than a response to those time pressures. Therefore, this is problem-focused coping because it attempts to deal directly with the stressor. In contrast, emotion-focused coping refers to how individuals manage their emotional reactions to stressors. Emotion-focused coping is exemplified when employees use avoidance or distancing behaviors in response to a stressor. For example, the person procrastinates or puts things off to the very last minute as a way of avoiding uncomfortable feelings. In other words, procrastination is just another word for coping indirectly. Such an individual says to themselves; "I'm running out of time," "What project should I do first?" or "Maybe I should go home sick." Many times, a person will continually spin in the stress cycle when there is no plan and goals for dealing directly with the stressor.

How people choose between the emotion-focused and problem-focused coping strategies is a significant factor in the experience of job stress. In essence, individuals are most likely to choose a strategy for coping if they believe it has the best chance of meeting the demands. The factor that seems to be fundamental in that decision tends to be the perception of how much control the individual feels in their current job context. People who feel they have control in their job environment are much more likely to use a problem-focused coping strategy to reduce the overall level of stress in the future. People that feel that they have less control in the situation on the job are much more likely to resort to the emotion-focused coping as the only realistic response that they have available. What determines whether people feel that they have a sense of control? Part of this is in the nature of the stressor itself. Frost (1983) argued that most job stress, described as role stress, comes from interpersonal interactions. Often dealing with people is what causes stress in the degree to which one feels a lost sense of control when dealing with that individual, which in turn complicates the task, the organization, the person's job title, and the culture of the organization.

Strain is a term used to describe the kinds of symptoms or responses that an individual feels in response to stressors and coping strategies. Some physiological strains may be related to the body's immune system, the cardiovascular system, musculoskeletal system, or even the gastrointestinal system. These types of strains might include stomachaches, headaches, increased blood pressure, and increased likelihood of becoming ill. Psychological strains include things like anxiety, depression, anger, reduced self-confidence, and irritability. There might be a relatively long list of psychological strains, but all of these can eventually lead to a phenomenon known as burnout. Burnout is a strain, in part constituted by emotional exhaustion, in part by a decreased sense of physical impact on the job, and in part by depersonalization or lack of empathy on the job (Maslach 1978). Now burnout was initially developed for social workers and those in such occupations as social work, where emotional management is a significant part of the work. However, many occupations now include emotional work, so burnout has become increasingly popular as a topic in many professions. Most managers today are vulnerable to burnout conditions.

Behavioral strains include unhealthy behaviors such as grinding of teeth, smoking tobacco, compulsive gum chewing, overuse of alcohol or drugs, and compulsive eating. While we know less about why individuals choose to engage in specific behavioral strain behaviors, it is, however, clear that it is undesirable, both from a personal and from the organization standpoint that individuals engage in unhealthy behaviors. One connection to behavioral strains is the so-called type A behavior pattern. Cardiologists Friedman and Rosenman (1959) developed type A behavior pattern in the 1950s while studying patients who have had significant cardiovascular disease. They identified those individuals who had a reoccurrence of the disease (e.g., a heart attack) and the researchers identified those patients as the A group. Patients who did not suffer a second attack were place in the B group. Researchers then interviewed the patients and sought out daily behaviors or habits that would occur in one group but not the other group. The results for the A group became the type A behavior pattern and it has a range of characteristics, but for our purposes, there was one set of behaviors that are most associated with continued heart disease. The unhealthy components are most linked to responses of inappropriate aggressiveness or to responses of unusually high competitiveness. In other words, stress responses activated too often and too long due to anger, frustration, or competitiveness on the job are unhealthy and should be avoided. Do not make the mistake of associating type A behavior only with a tendency to be sensitive to deadlines (e.g., trying to do more in less time). While that might be the most obvious or visible component of the type A behavior pattern, it indeed is not the unhealthy part of coping.

When considering the overall impact of strain social support is important too. Social support refers to the help people receive when they are confronted with stressful demands (Cooper, Dewe, and O'Driscoll 2001). There are many forms of social support; the two most important to us are called instrumental support and emotional support. Instrumental support refers to the help the person receives. It can be used to address the stressful demand directly as help might come in terms of information about the job, or it might come in the form of assistance or physically offering to help with the job. The second type, social support, is called emotional support in reference to the help the person receives in dealing with the emotional distress that accompanies the stressful demands. A supervisor that is empathetic and understanding is an excellent example of emotional support. A co-worker that allows the individual under stress to vent their emotional responses and discuss their frustrations is providing emotional, social support.

Social support in its various forms is a buffering factor in terms of job stress and strain relations (Viswesvaran, Sanchez, and Fisher 1999). A buffering factor means merely that the presence of social support will reduce or minimize the negative impacts of the perception of stress and its associated strain symptoms. For example, deadlines for one employee might be foundational to having a very stressful week, but the presence of a co-worker who will provide help or assistance to help meet those deadlines, plus an empathetic boss are both social support, in the form of instrumental support and emotional support. This effort may make the overall existence of that strain less stressful to cope with and the resulting strain, be it physiological, psychological, or behavioral, is significantly reduced. Clearly, workers perceive stress on the job as a negative relationship with job performance behaviors and organizational attitudes. However, it is clear from the aforementioned that the presence of stressors does not always lead to decreases in job performance or even in more negative job attitudes.

Resources Organizations Provide to Help Employees Cope With Job Stress

Employing organizations can and do conduct stress audits and respond by providing institutional level resources, including everything from health coaches to time off work to cope with the stress and the resulting strains. However, individuals need to respond on their own to work stressors as well, and that is our focus here. One means that an individual can engage in is a means of coping with stress to increase job-related competencies, skills, and satisfaction. Individuals with more competencies and skills can handle more demands before becoming overwhelmed by the demands of the stressors, thus increasing job satisfaction. Volunteering for or seeking out stress management programs, developing social networks, conflict resolution workshops, or workshops focusing on communication and assertiveness skills are excellent ideas.

A second way organizations provide resources to employees so that they can cope more effectively with job stress is through supportive practices. The first example of such a supportive practice might be flextime. An individual in an organization should take advantage of flextime, if available, but the concept of flextime is possible in any workplace and can be pursued individuals as well. Many organizations are allowing flextime, by creating compressed alternative work schedules such as 9/80s, which provide for three consecutive days off (e.g., five days of work followed by three days off, followed by four days of work followed by a single day off), or 4/10 work schedule, which provide three consecutive days off every week. Additionally, an employer might allow for the bringing of a child to work if needed. Other work schedule–related options might include job sharing, seeking part-time or full-time virtual work arrangements, or exploring on-site childcare opportunities.

An additional method for managing stressors is a strain reducing practice of learning relaxation skills. Relaxation skills might include progressive muscle relaxation, meditation, walking, writing in a journal, or just practicing deep breathing techniques (Manikonda et al. 2005). While these various methods involve different behaviors, they teach people how to counteract the effects of stressors by engaging in activities that slow the person's heart rate, their breathing rate, and potentially lowers their blood pressure. For example, Blue Cross Blue Shield of Tennessee has successfully trained many of 4,500 employees in biofeedback technology to reduce stress associated with financial uncertainties.

Some organizations provide stress-related training in cognitive-behavioral techniques. A popular example of this would be providing meditation rooms for employees to use during working hours. Other employers provide EAPs that conduct individual counseling sessions for stressed employees. More and more employers provide health and wellness programs as a benefit to employees (Ensel and Lin 2004). Health and wellness coaches, for example, may telephone employees weekly to support their chosen means of coping with job stressors. Even optimism (Taylor et al. 2000) and humor (Romero and Cruthirds 2006) can be psychological resources in the coping process.

Where Can Health Competence Be Developed?

Being aware of what employees encounter daily will assist a manager in his or her pursuit of a high-performance work team. Having all managers trained in the many facets of EAP, cognitive behavior techniques, health and wellness programs, employee safety, and health competencies may be a pie in the sky idea and yet, even that may not be enough if workplaces continue to be increasingly stressful. However, understanding and managing employee stressors will be the difference between leading and being a part of a fully functional organization or in being the head of a dysfunctional team.

To have a successful work team, the group's manager must recognize and minimize the number of stressors since this is the most direct way to minimize the total level of employee stress. The organization's leadership at all levels must fully understand the organization's, department's, and division's mission, vision, and goals. Individual employee must accept and adapt to the organizations' mission as well as their division's goals by participating in the development and or redevelopment and shepherding of those goals and objectives. Management must be held accountable for being the gatekeepers and path clearers for their staff. Doing so, along with facilitating, mentoring, and coaching, will produce a much less stressful working environment, allowing each employee to achieve job satisfaction, health, and wellness, and the ability to reduce or eliminate, in some cases, stressors and the byproducts thereof. In the final analysis, employee job satisfaction increases as well as improvements in worker safety occur, operating cost decreases, operational efficiencies increase, waste in processes is reduced if not in many cases, eliminated, and productivity is measurably increased when job stress becomes a central management concern.

Health Competence Readings[1]

For your reading pleasure and in support of this chapter's theme of health competence, the following book selections are intended to provide a list of tools readers may desire to try on or take for a spin around the block. Enjoy the read and know there is a vast amount of information just waiting to be discovered and used. Adding tools to life's toolbelts provides a sense of comfort in knowing when a problem arises, readers possess resolution tools that can be used to slay the fire breathing dragons cloaked in the guise of stress.

Powell, T.J., and S.J. Enright. 1990. *Anxiety and Stress Management.* London: Routledge, https://doi.org/10.4324/9781315683867

This book is for health care providers as well as individuals at any level of an organization working toward the management of stressful working environments. As the authors note, most stress is a normal part of daily life and can be coped with adequately by the individual. Prolonged or more severe stress, however, may require professional help. A local general practitioner (GP) can often provide this, but in many cases, they will refer the client to a mental health worker or other health professional. This book can be helpful to readers because it was written as a practical handbook and guide for those professionals working in the field of mental health but also written for the referring GP and those seeking help themselves.

The authors' major premise relating to anxiety and stress begins with a theoretical section offering a working model of stress, a guide to

---

[1] This section was written with the assistance of Vernice Haddix.

diagnostic classification, and alternative models of anxiety. This is followed by chapters on assessment, explaining the problem and treatment procedures to the client, teaching specific self-help skills, and changing stressful lifestyles. Advice is also given on running anxiety and stress management groups, and individual case studies are examined. The authors make extensive use of analogy and metaphor to ensure ready understanding and recall. They also include many useful inventories, questionnaires, charts, and client handouts.

Readers of this book should find utility in the way the authors have outlined the elements of effective instruction for identifying the issues from the cause through to solutions. *Anxiety and Stress Management* will be of use to all health professionals working with people who have anxiety and stress-related problems and will prove equally valuable for the clients themselves as a reference book and as a means of self-education and self-help.

Quick, J.C., T.A. Wright, J.A. Adkins, D.L. Nelson, and J.D. Quick. 2013. *Preventive Stress Management in Organizations*. Washington, DC: American Psychological Association. http://dx.doi. org/10.1037/10238-000

Preventive Stress Management in Organizations offers a comprehensive, orderly framework for practicing healthy preventive stress management. The book begins with a panoramic overview of the stress field from its medical and physiological origins in the early 1900s through its psychological elaborations during the second half of the century and its current application and practice in organizations.

The authors examine the sources of stress; the psychophysiology of the stress response and individual moderators that condition vulnerability for distress; the psychological, behavioral, and medical forms of personal distress; and the organizational costs of distress.

The usefulness of the book stems from its framework for preventive stress management that can be practiced by both organizations and individuals. Specific chapters examine methods and instruments for diagnosing organizational and individual stress; ways to redesign work and improve professional relationships; and methods for managing demands and stressors, altering how one responds to inevitable and necessary demands. Organizational and individual prevention methods are designed to enhance health and performance at work while averting the costs and discomfort of distress. Examples of healthy organizations are illustrated throughout the text, with specific case examples of implementing preventive management.

Seaward, B.L. 2017. *Managing Stress: Principles and Strategies for Health and Well-Being.* **Burlington, MA: Jones & Bartlett Learning. ISBN 9781284148589**

This book can be useful as an additional tool for student practitioners willing to learn another way of dealing with stress by using a comprehensive and interactive eBook named *Navigate 2 Advantage Access*. This tool will allow readers to practice activities and conduct assessments, along with a full suite of instructor resources, and learning analytics reporting tools.

The authors' major premise is that managing stress through the principles and strategies for health and well-being provides a comprehensive approach to stress management honoring the integration, balance, and harmony of mind, body, spirit, and emotions. The holistic approach taken by the author gently guides the reader to higher levels of mental, emotional, physical, and spiritual well-being by emphasizing the importance of mind–body–spirit unity.

This book gives students the tools needed to identify and manage stress while teaching them how to strive for health and balance while outlining elements of effective stress management alternatives.

McGonigal, K. 2016. *The Upside of Stress: Why Stress is Good for You, and How to Get Good at it.* **London: Penguin Books. ISBN 9781101982938**

Most studies on stress view the phenomena from the negative side of the scale, but contrary to that approach this book takes the approach that there is an upside to stress. This author offers a surprising new view of stress, one that reveals the upside of stress, and shows us exactly how to capitalize on its benefits.

This author poses the question that if stress causes heart disease, insomnia, and is bad for you; what if changing how you think about stress could make you happier, healthier, and better able to reach reader's goals? Combining exciting new research on resilience and mindset, the author Kelly McGonigal proves that undergoing stress is not bad for you; it is undergoing stress while believing that stress is bad for you that makes it harmful. Stress has many benefits, from giving us greater focus and energy to strengthening our personal relationships.

McGonigal shows readers how to cultivate a mindset that embraces stress and activate the brain's natural ability to learn from challenging experiences. Both practical and life-changing, *The Upside of Stress* is not a guide to getting rid of stress but a toolkit for getting better at it—by understanding, accepting, and leveraging it to your advantage. This book is useful to readers because it challenges the reader to be open-minded to the concepts of stress and to search outside the box for possible positive solutions.

Greenberger, D., and C.A. Padesky. 2015. *Mind over Mood: Change How You Feel by Changing the Way You Think.* **New York, NY: Guilford Publications.ISBN 9781462520428**

Another excellent book for employees at any level of an organization as is evident in the simple and yet powerful explanation of the steps that can be taken to overcome emotional distress to feel happier, calmer, and more confident. The authors state that the use of book has already helped more than 1.1 million readers become familiar with and to use cognitive-behavioral therapy (CBT)—one of today's most effective forms of psychotherapy—to conquer depression, anxiety, panic attacks, anger, guilt, shame, low self-esteem, stress, eating disorders, substance abuse, and relationship problems.

This book can be useful to readers in that it contains 60 worksheets and numerous new features: expanded content on anxiety; chapters on setting personal goals and maintaining progress; happiness rating scales; gratitude journals; innovative exercises focused on mindfulness, acceptance, and forgiveness.

The authors' major premise is that *Mind Over Mood* will help you do the following: learn proven and powerful practical strategies to transform lives; set doable personal goals and track progress, and by following step-by-step plans to overcome depression, anxiety, anger, guilt, and shame helps the user to sort out their thoughts, and to help one understand how their thoughts lead to feelings and behaviors. When it is realized it is their thoughts that are triggering feelings, irrational fears, and their often-harmful actions, then they can work on stopping the thoughts and produce for themselves improved life choices.

Ashkanasy, N., W. Zerbe, and C. Hartel. 2002. *Managing Emotions in the Workplace*. New York, NY: Routledge. https://doi. org/10.4324/9781315290812

This book brings to the forefront an understanding the individuals bring with them to work more than their lunches. Experiences, passion, and emotions accompany each person while they move about the workplace. Individuals bring their affected states and emotional "buttons" to work. Leaders do what they can, if trained, to engender feelings of passion and enthusiasm for the organization and its mission and contract with consultants as needed to assist in increasing job satisfaction, commitment, and trust.

The authors' major premise for this book is to advance the understanding of the causes and effects of emotions at work and extends existing theories to consider implications for the management of emotions. The international cast of authors examines the practical issues raised when organizations are studied as places where emotions are aroused, suppressed, used, and avoided. This book also joins the debate on how organizations and individuals ought to manage emotions in the workplace.

Managing Emotions in the Workplace is designed for use in courses in Organizational Behavior, Human Resource Management, or Organizational Development—any course in which the role of emotions in the workplace is a central concern but readers from all walks of life may find this book useful and an essential resource on the latest theory and practice in this emerging field.

Stranks, J. 2005. *Stress at Work*. New York, NY: Routledge. ISBN 9780080481180

This book brings a perspective of stress from outside of the United States, that is from the UK. Behavior similarities are as expected. Validating that challenges and stress in the workplace appear to be the same regardless of which side of the Atlantic one resides, the author says that people at work worry about all sorts of things, increasing competition for jobs, globalization, terrorism, "rationalization" of the organization's operations, looking after ageing parents and relatives, the threat of redundancy, annual appraisals, new technology, outsourcing of jobs to India and other Third World countries together with increased demands by employers for higher productivity.

An essential discussion revolved around information about workers being put under excessive pressure at certain times, to meet goals, attend meetings on time, learn new procedures and fit in with changes within the organization's culture. This can result in varying levels of stress. According to the United Kingdom's Health and Safety Executive (HSE), workplace stress is now the fastest growing cause of absenteeism from work.

This book can be useful to the readers because it was written as a guide for managers, human resources professionals, and safety reps. The emphasis of this book is to provide practical advice and solutions. The author provides simple tools to measure and assess stress and shows how to deal with a range of stress-creating workplace situations, such as bullying, harassment, and violence at work. The book also details how to implement a stress management system that complies with their new HSE Management Standards to avoid civil claims and criminal sanctions by the enforcement agencies. It should enable the reader to understand the meaning of stress, the causes of stress, human responses to stress, and aspects of behavior which are significant in this area. Employers need to manage stress by incorporating employee stress protection into their management systems.

References

Allen, T.D., L.T. Eby, M.L. Poteet, E. Lentz, and L. Lima. 2004. "Career Benefits Associated with Mentoring for Proteges: A Meta-Analysis." *Journal of Applied Psychology* 89, no. 1, pp. 127–136.

Alvesson, M., K.L. Ashcraft, and R. Thomas. 2008. "Identity Matters: Reflections on the Construction of Identity Scholarship in Organizational Studies." *Organization* 15, pp. 5–28.

Ang, S., L. Van Dyne, and C. Koh. 2004. *The Measurement of Cultural Intelligence. Paper presented at the Academy of Management Meeting's Symposium on Cultural Intelligence in the 21st Century.* New Orleans, LA.

Ang, S., L. Van Dyne, and C. Koh. 2006. "Personality Correlates of the Four-Factor Model of Cultural Intelligence." *Group and Organization Management* 31, pp. 100–123.

Armstrong, M. 2006. *A Handbook of Human Resource Management Practice,* 10th ed. Philadelphia, PA: Kogan Page Limited.

Ashforth, B.E., and F.A. Mael. 1989. "Social Identity Theory and the Organization." *Academy of Management Review* 14, pp. 20–39.

Ashkanasy, N., W. Zerbe, and C. Hartel. 2002. *Managing Emotions in the Workplace.* New York, NY: Routledge.

Austin, E.J., D. Farelly, C. Black, and H. Moore. 2007. "Emotional Intelligence, Machiavellianism and Emotional Manipulation: Does EI have a Dark Side?" *Personality & Individual Differences* 43, pp. 179–189.

Aycan, Z., R. Kanungo, M. Mendonca, K. Yu, J. Deller, G. Stahl, and A. Kurshid. 2000. "Impact of Culture on Human Resource Management Practice: A 10-Country Comparison." *Applied Psychology* 49, no. 1, pp. 192–221.

Bagby, R.M., J.D.A. Parker, and G.J. Taylor. 1994. "The Twenty-Item Toronto Alexithymia Scale: Part I, Item Selection and Cross-Validation of the Factor Structure." *Journal of Psychosomatic Research* 38, pp. 23–32.

Baldwin, T.T., and M.Y. Padgett. 1994. "Management Development: A Review and Commentary." In *Key Reviews in Managerial Psychology: Concepts and research for Practice,* eds. C.L. Cooper, I.T. Robertson, and Associates, 270–320. Chicester, UK: Wiley.

Bar-On, R. 1997. *Bar-On Emotional Quotient Inventory (EQ-i): A Test of Emotional Intelligence.* Toronto, Canada: Multi-Health Systems.

Bar-On, R., and J.D.A. Parker., eds. 2000. *The Handbook of Emotional Intelligence: Theory, Development, Assessment, and Application at Home, School, and in the Workplace.* San Francisco, CA: Jossey-Bass.

Bass, B.M. 1990. *Bass and Stogdill's Handbook of Leadership: Theory, Research, and Managerial Applications*. New York, NY: Free Press.

Bednar, J. February 15, 2010. "Beyond the 9-to-5." *Business West*, p. 18.

Benko, C., and M. Anderson. 2010. *The Corporate Lattice: Achieving High Performance in the Changing World of Work*. Boston, MA: Harvard Business School Press.

Berger, C.R., and J.J. Bradac. 1982. *Language and Social Knowledge: Uncertainty in Interpersonal Relations*. London: Edward Arnold.

Bhagat, R.S., B.L. Kedia, S.E. Crawford, and M.R. Kaplan. 1990. "Cross-Cultural Issues in Organizational Psychology: Emergent Trends and Directions for Research in the 1990s." *International Review of Industrial and Organizational Psychology* 5, no. 3, pp. 55–99.

Bhagat, R.S., J. Segovis, and T. Nelson. 2016. *Work Stress and Coping in the Era of Globalization*. New York, NY: Routledge.

Bluedorn, A.C. 1978. "A Taxonomy of Turnover." *Academy of Management Review* 3, pp. 647–651.

Bray, E.W., R.J. Campbell, and D.L. Grant. 1974. *Formative Years in Business: A Long-Term AT & T Study of Managerial Lives*. New York, NY: Wiley.

Brynjolfsson, E., J.J. Horton, A. Ozimek, D. Rock, G. Sharma, and H.Y. TuYe. 2020. COVID-19 and Remote Work: An Early Look at U.S. Data (No. w27344). National Bureau of Economic Research.

Caruso, D.R., J.D. Mayer, and P. Salovey. 2002. "Emotional Intelligence and Emotional Leadership." In *Multiple Intelligences and Leadership*, eds. R.E. Riggio, S.E. Murphy, and F.J. Pirozzalo, 55–74. Mahwah, NJ: Lawrence Erlbaum.

Chakravarthy, B.S., and H.V. Perlmutter. 1992. "Strategic Planning for a Global Business." In *International Strategic Management: Challenges and Opportunities*, eds. H. Vernon-Wortzel and L.H. Wortzel, 29–42. New York, NY: Taylor & Francis.

Chen, M. 2001. *Inside Chinese Business*. Boston, MA: Harvard Business School Press.

Cheney, G. 1991. *Rhetoric in an Organizational Society: Managing Multiple Identities*. Columbia, SC: University of South Carolina Press.

Cherniss, C. 2004. "The Business Case for Emotional Intelligence." *Consortium for Research on Emotional Intelligence in Organizations*. Available from http://eiconsortium.org/research/business-case-for-ei.htm

Chien Farh, C.I.C., M.G. Seo, and P.E. Tesluk. 2012. "Emotional Intelligence, Teamwork Effectiveness, and Job Performance: The Moderating Role of Job Context." *Journal of Applied Psychology* 97, no. 4, pp. 890–900.

Ciarrochi, J., J.P. Forgas, and J.D. Mayer., eds. 2001. *Emotional Intelligence in Everyday Life*. Philadelphia, PA: Psychology Press.

Clark, L.A., and K.S. Lyness. 1991. "Succession Planning as a Strategic Activity at Citicorp." In *Advances in Applied Business Strategy*, ed. L.W. Foster, Vol. 2. Greenwich, CT: JAI Press.

Conlin, M. 2007. "Go-Go-Going to pieces in China." *Business Week* 88, p. 4031." Available from https://bloomberg.com/news/articles/2007-04-22/go-go-going-to-pieces-in-china

Conte, J.M. 2005. "A Review and Critique of Emotional Intelligence Measures." *Journal of Organizational Behavior* 26, no. 4, pp. 433–440.

Cooper, R.K. 1997. "Applying Emotional Intelligence in the Workplace." *Training and Development* 51, no. 12, pp. 31–39.

Cooper, C.L., P.J. Dewe, and M.P. O'Driscoll. 2001. *Organizational Stress: A Review and Critique of Theory, Research, and Applications.* Thousand Oaks, CA: Sage.

Cote, S., and C.T.H. Miners. 2006. "Emotional Intelligence, Cognitive Intelligence, and Job Performance." *Administrative Science Quarterly* 51, no. 1, pp. 1–28.

Crock, S. November 24, 2003. "Collaborative Lockheed Martin." *Business Week*, p. 85.

Day, D.V. 2001. "Leadership Development: A Review in Context." *Leadership Quarterly* 11, no. 4, pp. 581–613.

Dechant, K. 1994. "Making the Most of Job Assignments: An Exercise in Planning for Learning." *Journal of Management Education* 18, pp. 198–211.

Decker, T. 2003. "Is Emotional Intelligence a Viable Concept?" *Academy of Management Review* 28, no. 2, pp. 433–440.

Dragoni, L., P.E. Tesluk, J.E.A. Russell, and I. Oh. 2009. "Understanding Managerial Development: Integrating Developmental Assignments, Learning Orientation, and Access to Developmental Opportunities in Predicting Managerial Competencies." *Academy of Management Journal* 52, no. 4, pp. 731–743.

Duarte, D.L., and N.T. Snyder. 2001. *Mastering Virtual Teams*, 2nd ed. San Francisco, CA: Jossey-Bass.

Dube, L., and D. Robey. 2007. "Surviving the Paradoxes of Virtual Teamwork." *Informational Systems Journal* 19, no. 1, pp. 3–30.

Elfenbein, H.A., and N. Ambady. 2002. "Predicting Workplace Outcomes from the Ability to Eavesdrop on Feelings." *Journal of Applied Psychology* 87, no. 5, pp. 963–971.

Encyclopedia of Mathematics. 2020. "Law of Large Numbers." Retrieved from http://Encylcopediaofmath.org/index.php?title=Law-of-large-numbers+oldid=26552

Ensel, W.M., and N. Lin. 2004. "Physical Fitness and the Stress Response." *Journal of Community Psychology* 32, no. 1, pp. 81–101.

Fallacy Files. n.d. "The Base Rate Fallacy." Available from www.fallacyfiles.org/baserate.html

Feldman, D.C. 1976. "A Contingency Theory of Socialization." *Administrative Science Quarterly* 211, pp. 433–452.

Fiedler, F.E. 1967. *A Theory of Leadership Effectiveness*. New York, NY: McGraw-Hill.

Fiedler, F.E. 1978. "The Contingency Model and the Dynamics of the Leadership Process." In *Advances in Experimental Social Psychology*, ed. L. Berkowitz, 11, 59–112. New York, NY: Academic Press.

Fiedler, F.E., M.M. Chemers, and L. Mahar. 1976. *Improving Leadership Effectiveness: The Leader Match Concept*. New York: Wiley.

Fischhoff, B. 1975. "Hindsight≠Foresight: The Effect of Outcome Knowledge on Judgment Under Uncertainty." *Journal of Experimental Psychology: Human Perception and Performance* 1, no. 3, pp. 288–299.

Fischhoff, B. 1982. "Debiasing." In *Judgment Under Uncertainty: Heuristics and Biases*, eds. D. Kahneman, P. Slovic, and A. Tversky. Cambridge, UK: Cambridge University Press.

Fischhoff, B., P. Slovic, and S. Lichtenstein. 1977. "Knowing with Certainty: The Appropriateness of Extreme Confidence." *Journal of Experimental Psychology: Human Perception and Performance* 3, no. 4, pp. 552–564.

Fleishman, E.A. 1957. "A Leader Behavior Description for Industry." In *Leader Behavior: Its Description and Measurement*, eds. R.M. Stogdill and A.E. Coons.. Columbus, OH: Ohio State University, Bureau of Business Research.

Foa, U.G., and E.B. Foa. 1980. "Resource Theory: Interpersonal Behavior as Exchange." In *Social Exchange: Advances in Theory and Research*, eds. K.J. Gergen, M.S. Greenberg, and R.H. Willis, eds. 77–94. New York, NY: Plenum.

Folkman, S., R.S. Lazarus, C. Dunkel-Schetter, A. De Longis, and R.J. Gruen. 1986. "Dynamics of a Stressful Encounter: Cognitive Appraisal, Coping, and Encounter Outcomes." *Journal of Personality and Social Psychology* 50, no. 5, pp. 992–1003.

Freud, S. 1996. *Three Case Histories*, 132. New York, NY: Touchstone.

Friedman, M., and R. Rosenman. 1959. "Association of Specific Overt Behavior Pattern with Blood and Cardiovascular Findings." *Journal of the American Medical Association* 169, no. 12, pp. 1286–1296.

Frost, D.E. 1983. "Role Perceptions and Behavior of the Immediate Superior: Moderating Effects on the Prediction of Leadership Effectiveness." *Organizational Behavior and Human Performance* 31, pp. 123–142.

Frost, D.E. 2004. "The Psychological Measurement of Emotional Intelligence." In *Comprehensive Handbook of Psychological Assessment*, eds. M. Hersen and J. Thomas, Vol 4, 203–215. New York, NY: Wiley.

Frost, D.E., and V. Wallingford. 2013. "Experiential Learning for Developing

Managers: A Practical Model." *Journal of Management Development* 32, no. 7, pp. 756–767.

Frost, D.E. 2021. *Strategic Management.* Dubuque, IA: Kendall Hunt Publishing.

Frost, P.J., L.F. Moore, M.R. Louis, C.C. Lundberg, and J. Martin. 1991. *Reframing Organizational Culture.* Newbury Park, CA: Sage Publications.

Galinsky, E. 2005. *Overwork in America: When the Way We Work Becomes Too Much.* New York, NY: Families and Work Institute.

Gambrel, P.A., and R. Cianci. 2003. "Maslow's Hierarchy of Needs: Does it Apply in a Collectivist Culture?" *Journal of Applied Management and Entrepreneurship* 8, no. 2, pp. 143–161.

Gardner, H. 1983. *Frames of Mind: The Theory of Multiple Intelligences.* New York, NY: Basic Books.

George, J.M. 2000. "Emotions and Leadership: The Role of Emotional Intelligence." *Human Relations* 53, pp. 1027–1055.

Gibbs, J.L., A. Sivunen, and M. Boyraz. 2017. "Investigating the Impacts of Team Type and Design on Virtual Team Processes." *Human Resource Management Review* 27, pp. 590–603.

Gibson, C.B., and S.G. Cohen. 2003. *Virtual Teams that Work: Creating Conditions for Virtual Team Effectiveness.* San Francisco, CA: Jossey-Bass.

Gilovich, T., R. Vallone, and A. Tversky. 1985. "The Hot Hand in Basketball: On the Misinterpretation of Random Sequences." *Cognitive Psychology* 17, no. 3, pp. 295–314.

Golden, T.D., and Veiga, J.F. 2008. "The Impact of Superior-Subordinate Relationships on the Commitment, Job Satisfaction, and Performance of Virtual Workers." *The Leadership Quarterly* 19, pp. 77–88.

Goleman, D. 1995. *Emotional Intelligence.* New York, NY: Bantam.

Goleman, D. 1999. *Working with Emotional Intelligence.* New York, NY: Bantam.

Graen, G.B., and M. Uhl-Bien. 1995. "Relationship-Based Approach to Leadership: Development of Leader-Member Exchange (LMX) Theory of Leadership over 25 years: Applying a Multi-Domain Perspective." *Leadership Quarterly* 6, no. 2, pp. 219–247.

Grant-Vallone, E.J., and S.I. Donaldson. 2001. "Consequences of Work-Family Conflict on Employee Well-Being Over Time." *Work & Stress* 15, no. 3, pp. 214–226.

Greenberger, D., and C.A. Padesky. 2015. *Mind Over Mood: Change How You Feel by Changing the Way You Think.* New York, NY: Guilford Publications.

Grudykunst, W.B., M.R. Hammer, and R.L. Wiseman. 1977. "An Analysis of an Integrated Approach to Cross-Cultural Training." *International Journal of Intercultural Relations* 1, no. 2, pp. 99–110.

Haire, M., E.E. Ghiselli, and L.W. Porter. 1966. *Managerial Thinking: An International Study.* New York: Wiley.

Hardman, D.K., and D. Hardman. 2009. *Judgment and Decision Making: Psychological Perspectives.* Malden, MA: Wiley.

Harris, P.R., and R.T. Moran. 1991. *Managing Cultural Differences*, 3rd ed. Houston, TX: Gulf Publishing.

Harrison, E.F. 1999. *The Managerial Decision Making Process*, 5th ed. Boston, MA: Houghton-Mifflin.

Harwood, G.G. 2008. "Design Principles for Successful Virtual Teams." In *The Handbook of High-Performance Virtual Teams: A Toolkit for Collaborating Across Boundaries*, eds. J. Nemiro and M.M. Beyerlein. San Francisco, CA: Jossey-Bass.

Heider, F. 1958. *The Psychology of Interpersonal Relations.* New York, NY: Wiley.

Hemphill, J.K. 1950. *Leader Behavior Description.* Columbus, OH: Ohio State Personnel Research Board.

Hersey, P., and K.H. Blanchard. 1974. "So You Want to Know Your Leadership Style?" *Training and Development Journal* 28, no. 2, pp. 22–37.

Hertel, G., S. Geister, and U. Konradt. 2005. "Managing Virtual Teams: A Review of Ccurrent Empirical Research." *Human Resource Management Review* 15, pp. 69–95.

Hill, E.J., J.J. Erickson, E.K. Holmes, and M. Ferris. 2010. "Workplace Flexibility, Work Hours, and Work-Life Conflict: Finding an Extra Day or Two." *Journal of Family Psychology* 24, no 3, pp. 349–358.

Hirsh, W., and A. Carter. 2202. *New Directions in Management Development.* Brighton, UK: Institute for Employment Studies.

Hoch, J.E., and S.W.J. Kozlowski. 2014. "Leading virtual teams: Hierarchical leadership, structural supports, and shared team leadership." *Journal of Applied Psychology* 99, no. 3, pp. 390–403.

Hodgetts, R.M. 2002. *Modern Human Relations at Work*, 5th ed. Fort Worth, TX: Harcourt.

Hoecklin, L. 1995. *Managing Cultural Differences: Strategies for Competitive Advantage.* Workingham, UK: Addison-Wesley.

Hofstede, G. 1972. "The Colors of Collars." *Columbia Journal of World Business* 7, no. 5, pp. 72–80.

Hofstede, G. 1980. *Cultures Consequences: International Differences in Work-Related Values.* Beverly Hills, CA: Sage.

Hofstede, G. 1991. "Empirical Models of Cultural Differences." In *Contemporary Issues in Cross-Cultural Psychology*, eds. N. Bleichredt and P.J.D. Drenth, 4–20. Amsterdam, Netherlands: Swets & Zeitlinger Publishers.

Hofstede, G.J. 2009. "Research on Cultures: How to Use it in Training." *European Journal of Cross-Cultural Competence and Management* 1, no. 1, pp. 14–21.

Hofstede, G., G.J. Hofstede, and M. Minkov. 2005. *Cultures and Organizations: Software of the Mind.* New York: McGraw-Hill.

House, R.J. 1971. "A Path-Goal Theory of Leadership Effectiveness." *Administrative Science Quarterly* 16, no. 3, pp. 321–338.

House, R.J. 1996. "Path-Goal Theory of Leadership: Lessons, Legacy, and a Reformulated Theory." *Leadership Quarterly* 7, no. 3, pp. 323–352.

House, R., P.J. Hanges, M. Javidan, P.W. Dorfman, and V. Gupta. 2004. *Culture, Leadership, and Organizations: The GLOBE Study of 62 Societies.* London: Sage.

House, R., and R. Mitchell. 1974. "Path-Goal Theory of Leadership." *Journal of Contemporary Business* 3, pp. 81–97.

Howard, A., and D.W. Bray. 1988. *Managerial Lives in Transition: Advancing Age and Changing Times.* New York, NY: Guilford Press.

Humphrey, R.H. 2002. "The Many Faces of Emotional Leadership." *The Leadership Quarterly* 13, no. 5, pp. 493–504.

Jablin, F.M. 1987. "Organizational Entry, Assimilation, and Exit." In *Handbook of Organizational Communication: An Interdisciplinary Perspective*, eds. F.M. Jablin, L.L. Putnam, K.H. Roberts, and L.W. Porter, 679–740. Newbury Park, CA: Sage.

Jablin, F.M. 2001. "Organizational Entry, Assimilation, and Disengagement/ Exit." In *The New Handbook of Organizational Communication: Advances in Theory, Research, and Methods*, F.M. Jablin and L.L. Putnam, 732–818. Thousand Oaks, CA: Sage.

Jackson, S.E., R.S. Schuler, and S. Werner. 2016. *Managing Human Resources.* Boston, MA: South-Western Cengage Learning.

Jones, E, and R.E. Nisbett. 1987. "The Actor and the Observer: Divergent Perceptions of the Causes of Behavior." In *Attribution: Perceiving the Causes of Behavior*, eds. E.E. Jones, D.E. Kanouse, H. H. Kelley, R.E. Nisbett, S. Valins, and B. Weiner, 79–94. Mahwah, NJ: Lawrence Erlbaum Associates.

Joseph, D.L., J. Jin, D.A. Newman, and E.H. O'Boyle. 2015. "Why Does Self-Reported Emotional Intelligence Predict Job Performance? A Meta-Analytic Investigation of Mixed EI." *Journal of Applied Psychology* 100, no. 2, pp. 298–342.

Joseph, D.L., and D.A. Newman. 2010. 'Emotional Intelligence: An Integrative Meta-Analysis and Cascading Model." *Journal of Applied Psychology* 95, no. 1, pp. 54–78.

Joynt, P., and M. Warner. 1996. *Managing Across Cultures: Issues and Perspectives.* London: International Thomson Business Press.

Judge, T.A., R.R. Piccolo, and R. Illies. 2004. "The Forgotten Ones? The Validity of Consideration and Initiating Structure in Leadership Research." *Journal of Applied Psychology* 89, pp. 36–51.

Kahneman, D. 2003. "Maps of Bounded Rationality: Psychology for Behavioral Economics." *The Economic Review* 93, no. 5, pp. 1449–1475.

Kahneman, D. 2011. *Thinking, Fast and Slow.* New York, NY: Farrar, Strauss, and Giroux.

Kahneman, D., P. Slovic, and A. Tversky. eds. 1982. *Judgment Under Uncertainty: Heuristics and Biases.* Cambridge, UK: Cambridge University Press.

Kahneman, D., and A. Tversky. 1972. "Subjective Probability: A Judgment of Representativeness." *Cognitive Psychology* 3, no. 3, pp. 430–454.

Katz, D., and R.L. Kahn. 1978. *The Social Psychology of Organizations.* New York, NY: Wiley.

Kerr, S., and J. Jermier. 1978. "Substitutes for Leadership: Their Meaning and Measurement." *Organizational Behavior and Human Performance* 22, pp. 374–403.

Kerr, R., J. Garvin, N. Heaton, and E. Boyle. 2005. "Emotional Intelligence and Leadership Effectiveness." *Leadership & Organization Development Journal* 27, no. 4, pp. 265–279.

Keys, J.B., and J. Wolfe. 1988. "Management Education and Development: Current Issues and Emerging Trends." *Journal of Management* 16, pp. 307–336.

Kirkpatrick, S.A., and E.A. Locke. 1991. "Leadership: Do Traits Matter?" *Academy of Management Perspectives* 5, no. 2, pp. 48–60.

Kluckhorn, F. R., and F.L. Strodbeck. 1961. *Variations in Value Orientations.* New York, NY: Row, Peterson.

Kluemper, D.H., A. Mitra, and S. Wang. 2016. "Social media use in HRM." *Research in Personnel and Human Resource Management* 34, pp. 153–207.

Kramer, M.W. 2004. *Managing Uncertainty in Organizational Communication.* Mahwah, NJ: Lawrence Erlbaum.

Kramer, M.W. 2010. *Organizational Socialization: Joining and Leaving Organizations.* Cambridge, UK: Polity Press.

LeBoeuf, R.A. 2002. "Rationality." In *Annual Review of Psychology,* eds. S.T. Fiske, D.L. Schacter, and C. Zahn-Waxler, Vol 53, 491–517. Palo Alto, CA: Annual Review.

Law, K.S., C. Wong, and L.J. Song. 2004. "The Construct and Criterion Validity of Emotional Intelligence and Its Potential Utility for Management Studies." *Journal of Applied Psychology* 89, no. 3, pp. 483–496.

Lazarus, R.S. 2006. *Stress and Emotion: A New Synthesis.* New York, NY: Springer.

Lepak, D.P., and S.A. Snell. 1999. "The Human Resource Architecture: Toward a Theory of Human Capital Allocation and Development." *Academy of Management Review* 24, pp. 31–48.

Lester, W. December 20, 2006. "Poll: Stress Know Few Boundaries for People in Industrial Democracies." *USA Today.*

Lichtenstein, S., and B. Fischhoff. 1977. "Do Those Who Know More also Know More About How Much They Know?" *Organizational Behavior and Human Performance* 20, no. 2, pp. 159–183.

Lipnack, J., and J. Stamps. 2000. *Virtual Teams: People Working Across Boundaries with Technology*. New York, NY: Wiley.

Liptak, J.J., and E. Leutenberg. 2006. *Coping with Stress in the Workplace Workbook*. Duluth, MN: Whole Person Associates.

Locke, E.A. 2005. "Why Emotional Intelligence is an Invalid Concept." *Journal of Organizational Behavior* 26, no. 4, pp. 425–431.

Lord, R.G., C.L. DeVader, and G.M. Alliger. 1986. "A Meta-Analysis of the Relation Between Personality Traits and Leadership Perceptions: An Application of Validity Generalization Procedures." *Journal of Applied Psychology* 71, no. 3, pp. 402–410.

Louis, M.R. 1980. "Surprise and Sense Making: What Newcomers Experience in Entering Unfamiliar Organizational Settings." *Administrative Science Quarterly* 25, pp. 226–251.

Luthans, F., and J.P. Doh. 2015. *International Management: Culture, Strategy, and Behavior*, 9th ed. New York, NY: McGraw-Hill.

Luthans, F., P.A. Marsnik, P, and K.W. Luthans. 1997. "A Contingency Matrix Approach to IHRM." *Human Resource Management* 36, no. 2, pp. 183–199.

Mabey, C., and A. Thomson. 2001. *Achieving Management Excellence: A Survey of UK Management Development at the Millennium*. London, U.K.: Institute of Management.

Malhotra, A., A. Majchrzak, and B. Rosen. 2007. "Leading Virtual Teams." *Academy of Management Perspectives* 21, no. 1, pp. 60–70.

Manikonda, P., S. Stoerk, S. Tuegel, F. Schardt, C. Angermann, I. Gruenberger, O. Fuchs, H. Faller, and W. Voelker. 2005. "Influence of Non-Pharmacological Treatment (Contemplative, Meditation, and Breathing Techniques) on Stress Induced Hypertension: A Randomized Controlled Study." *American Journal of Hypertension* 18, no. 5, Supplement 1, pp. A89–90.

Mannix, E, and M.A. Neale. 2005. "What Differences Make a Difference? The Promise and Reality of Diverse Teams in Organizations." *Psychological Sciences in the Public Interest* 6, no. 2, pp. 31–55.

March, J.G., and H.A. Simon. 1958. *Organizations*. New York: Wiley.

Marlow, S.L., C.N. Lacerenza, J. Paoletti, C.S. Burke, and E. Salas. 2018. "Does Team Communication Represent a One-Size-Fits-All Approach? A Meta-Analysis of Team Communication and Performance." *Organizational Behavior and Human Decision Processes* 144, pp. 145–170.

Martins, L.L., L.L. Gilson, and M.T. Maynard. 2004. "Virtual Teams: What Do We Know and Where Do We Go From Here?" *Journal of Management* 30, no. 6, pp. 805–835.

Maslach, C. 1978. "Job Burnout: How People Cope." *Public Welfare* 36, no. 2, pp. 56–58.

Maslow, A. 1954. *Motivation and Personality*. New York, NY: Harper & Row.

Maslow, A.H. 1943. "A Theory of Human Motivation." *Psychological Review* 50, no. 4, pp. 370–396.

Mathis, R.L., and J.H. Jackson. 2011. *Human Resource Management: Essential Perspectives.* Boston, MA: Cengage Learning.

Mayer, J.D., P. Salovey, and D.R. Caruso. 1999. *MSCEIT Item Booklet.* Toronto, Canada: Multi-Health Systems.

Mayer, J.D., and P. Salovey. 1997. "What is Emotional Intelligence?" *Emotional Development and Emotional Intelligence: Educational Implications* 3, p. 31.

McCall, M.W. 2004. "Leadership Development through Experience." *Academy of Management Executive* 18, no. 3, pp. 127–130.

McCall, M.W., M.M. Lombardo, and A.M. Morrison. 1988. *The Lessons of Experience: How Successful Executives Develop on the Job.* Lexington, MA: Lexington Books.

McCauley, C.D., I.J. Eastman, and P.J. Ohlott. 1995. "Linking Management Selection and Development through Stretch Assignments." *Human Resource Management* 34, no. 1, pp. 93–115.

McCauley, C.D., M.N. Ruderman, P.J. Ohlott, and J.E. Morrow. 1994. "Assessing the Developmental Components of Managerial Jobs." *Journal of Applied Psychology* 79, no. 4, pp. 544–560.

McCloskey, D.W., and M. Igbaria. 2003. "Does Out of Sight Mean Out of Mind? An Empirical Investigation of the Career Advancement Prospects of Telecommuters." *Information Resources Management Journal* 16, pp. 19–34.

McGonigal, K. 2016. *The Upside of Stress: Why Stress is Good for You, and How to Get Good at it.* London, U.K.: Penguin Books.

McShane, S.L., and M.A. Von Glinow. 2013. *Organizational Behavior: Emerging Knowledge, Global Reality,* 6th ed. New York, NY: McGraw-Hill.

Mead, R. 1994. *International Management: Cross-Cultural Dimensions.* Cambridge, MA: Blackwell.

Meinert, D.H. June 2011. "Making Telecommuting Pay Off." *HR Magazine,* p. 33.

Mendenhall, M.E., and G. Oddou. 1985. "The Dimensions of Expatriate Acculturation: A Review." *Academy of Management Review* 10, no. 1, pp. 39–47.

Milkman, K.L., D. Chugh, and M.H. Brazerman. 2009. "How can Decision Making be Improved?" *Perspectives on Psychological Science* 4, no. 4, pp. 379–383.

Mintzberg, H. 1973. *The Nature of Managerial Work.* New York, NY: Harper & Row.

Mintzberg, H. 1996. "Musings on Management: Ten Ideas Designed to Rile Everyone Who Cares About Management." *Harvard Business Review* 74, no. 4, pp. 61–67.

Mohrman, S.A., S.G. Cohen, and A.M. Mohrman. 1995. *Designing Team-Based Organizations: New Forms for Knowledge Work.* San Francisco, CA: Jossey-Bass.

Moregeson, F.P., and S.E. Humphrey. 2006. "The Work Design Questionnaire (WDQ): Developing and Validating a Comprehensive Measure for Assessing Job Design and the Nature of Work." *Journal of Applied Psychology* 91, pp. 1321–1339.

Murray, M. 2002. *Beyond the Myths and Magic of Mentoring: How to Facilitate an Effective Mentoring Process.* New York, NY: Wiley.

Murray, M. 2012. "MBA Share in the U.S. Graduate Management Education Market." *Business Education & Administration* 3, no. 1, pp. 29–40.

Nelson, D.L., and C. Sutton. 1990. "Chronic Work Stress and Coping: A Longitudinal Study and Suggested New Directions." *Academy of Management Journal* 33, no. 4, pp. 859–869.

O'Boyle, E.H., R.H. Humphrey, J.M. Pollak, T.H. Hawver, and P.A. Story. 2011. "The Relation Between Emotional Intelligence and Job Performance: A Meta-Analysis." *Journal of Organizational Behavior* 32, no. 5, pp. 788–818.

Ohlott, P.J. 1998. "Job Assignments." In *Center for Creative Leadership Handbook of Leadership Development*, eds. C.D. McCauley, R.S. Moxley, and E. Van Velso, 127–159. San Francisco, CA: Jossey-Bass.

Oreg, S. 2003. "Resistance to Change: Developing an Individual Differences Measure." *Journal of Applied Psychology* 88, no. 4, pp. 680–693.

Pal, G.C. 2007. "Is there a Universal Self-Serving Bias?" *Psychological Sciences* 52, no. 1, pp. 85–89.

Paul, R., and L. Elder. 2001. *Critical Thinking: Tools for Taking Charge of Your Learning and Your Life.* Upper Saddle River, NJ: Prentice-Hall.

Panchak, P. October 2004. "Production Workers Can be your Competitive Edge." *Industry Week*, p. 11.

Pearson, C.M., and C.L. Porath. 2005. "On the Nature, Consequences, and Remedies of Workplace Incivility: No Time for 'Nice'? Think Again." *Academy of Management Executive* 19, no. 1, pp. 7–18.

Pedler, M., J. Burgoyne, and C. Brook. 2005. "What has Action Learning Learned to Become?" *Action Learning: Research and Practice* 2, no. 1, pp. 49–68.

Piaget, J. 1972. *The Psychology of Intelligence.* Totowa, NJ: Littlefield Adams.

Plous, S. 1993. *The Psychology of Judgment and Decision Making.* New York, NY: McGraw-Hill.

Plutchik, R. 2001. "The Nature of Emotions: Human Emotions have Deep Evolutionary Roots, A Fact that May Explain their Complexity and Provide Tools for Clinical Practice." *American Scientist* 89, no. 4, pp. 344–350.

Powell, T.J., and S.J. Enright. 1990. *Anxiety and Stress Management.* London, U.K.: Routledge.

Quick, J.C. 1997. *Preventive Stress Management in Organizations.* Washington, DC: American Psychological Association.

Quick, J.C., T.A. Wright, J.A. Adkins, D.L. Nelson, and J.D. Quick. 2013. *Preventive Stress Management in Organizations.* Washington, DC: American Psychological Association.

Quinn, R.E., S.R. Faerman, M.P. Thompson, M.R. McGrath, and D.S. Bright. 2015. *Becoming a Master Manager: A Competing Values Approach,* 6th ed. Hoboken, NJ: Wiley.

Raghuram, S., R. Garud, B. Wiesenfeld, and V. Gupta. 2001. "Factors Contributing to Virtual Work Adjustment." *Journal of Management* 27, pp. 383–405.

Rigby, D. 1998. *Management Tools and Techniques.* Boston, MA: Bain and Company.

Robbins, S.P., and T.A. Judge. 2017. *Organizational Behavior,* 17th ed. London, UK: Pearson.

Romero, E.J., and K.W. Cruthirds. 2006. "The Use of Humor in the Workplace." *Academy of Management Perspectives* 20, no. 2, pp. 58–69.

Rosete, D., and J. Ciarrochi. 2005. "Emotional Intelligence and its Relationship to Workplace Performance Outcomes of Leadership Effectiveness." *Leadership & Organization Development Journal* 26, no. 5, pp. 388–399.

Rothwell, W.J., and H.C. Kazanas. 1994. "Management Development: The State of the Art as Perceived by HRD Professionals." *Performance Improvement Quarterly* 4, no. 1, pp. 40–59.

Salovey, P., and J.D. Mayer. 1989. "Emotional Intelligence." *Imagination, Cognition, and Personality* 9, pp. 185–211.

Scarr, S. 1989. "Protecting General Intelligence: Constructs and Consequences for Interventions." In *Intelligence: Measurement, Theory, and Public Policy,* ed. R.L. Linn. Urbana, IL: University of Illinois Press.

Schien, E.H. 2004. Organizational Culture and Leadership. San Francisco, CA: Jossey-Bass.

Schriesheim, C.A., and L. Neider. 1996. "Path-Goal Theory of Leadership: The Long and Winding Road." *Leadership Quarterly* 7, no. 3, pp. 317–321.

Schutte, N.S., J.M. Malouff, L.E. Hall, D.J. Haggerty, J.T. Cooper, C.J. Golden, and L. Dornheim. 1998. "Development and Validation of a Measure of Emotional Intelligence." *Personality and Individual Differences* 25, pp. 167–177.

Seaward, B.L. 2017. *Managing Stress: Principles and Strategies for Health and Well-Being.* Burlington, MA: Jones & Bartlett Learning.

Shah, A.K., and D.M. Oppenheimer. 2008. "Heuristics Made Easy: An Effort-Reduction Framework." *Psychological Bulletin* 134, no. 2, pp. 207–222.

Shaw, M.E. 1981. *Group Dynamics: The Psychology of Small Group Behavior.* New York, NY: McGraw-Hill.

Shen, J. 2005. "International Training and Management Development: Theory and Reality." *Journal of Management Development* 24, no. 7, pp. 656–666.

Simon, H.A. 1972. "Theories of Bounded Rationality." In *Decision and Organization*, eds. C.B. McGuire & R. Radnor, 161–176. Amsterdam, Netherlands: North Holland Publishing.

Simon, H.A. 1979. "Rational Decision Making in Business Organizations." *The American Economic Review* 69, no. 4, pp. 493–513.

Simon, H.A. 1986. "Rationality in Psychology and Economics." In *Rational Choice*, eds. R.M. Hogarth and M.W. Reder. Chicago, IL: University of Chicago Press.

Spielberger, C.D., and E.C. Reheiser. 1994. "The Job Stress Survey: Measuring Gender Differences in Occupational Stress." *Journal of Social Behavior and Personality* 9, no. 2, pp. 199–218.

Stanovich, K.E., and R.F. West. 2000. "Individual Differences in Reasoning: Implications for The rationality Debate." *Behavioral & Brain Sciences* 23, pp. 645–665.

Staw, B.M. 1997. "The Escalation of Commitment: An Update and Appraisal." In *Organizational Decision Making*, ed. Z. Shapira. 191–215. New York, NY: Cambridge University Press.

Sternberg, R.J. 1988. *The Triarchic Mind: A New Theory of Human Intelligence.* New York, NY: Viking.

Stogdill, R.M. 1948. "Personal Factors Associated with Leadership: A Survey of the Literature." *The Journal of Psychology* 25, pp. 35–71.

Stogdill, R.M., and A.E. Coons. 1951. *Leader Behavior: Its Description and Measurement.* Columbus, OH: Ohio State University Bureau of Business Research.

Stranke, J. 2005. *Stress at Work.* New York, NY: Routledge.

Taylor, S.E., M.E. Kemeny, G.M. Reed, J.E. Bower, and T.L. Gruenwald. 2000. "Psychological Resources, Positive Illusions, and Health." *American Psychologist*, 55, no. 1, pp. 99–109.

Thibaut, J.W., and H.H. Kelley. 1959. The Social Psychology of Groups. New York, NY: John Wiley.

Toplak, M.E., R.F. West, and K.E. Stanovich. 2011. "The Cognitive Reflection Test as a Predictor of Performance on Heuristics-and-Biases Tasks." *Memory and Cognition,* 39, pp. 1275–1289.

Trompenaars, F., and C. Hampden-Turner. 1998. *Riding Waves of Culture: Understanding Diversity in Global Business,* 2nd ed. New York, NY: McGraw-Hill.

Tsai, C. 2011. "International Pay and Compensation." In *International Human Resource Management: Globalization, Natural Systems, and Multinational Companies,* eds. T. Edwards and C. Rees, 230–251, 3rd ed. Harlow, UK: Pearson Education Limited.

Tuerluin, B., N. Smits, E.P. Brouwers, and H.C. de Vet. 2016. "The Four-Dimensional Symptom Questionnaire (4DSQ) in the General Population,

Scale Structure, Reliability, Measurement Invariance and Normative Data: A Cross-Sectional Study." *Health and Quality of Life Outcomes* 14, pp. 1–16.

Tversky, A., and D. Kahneman. 1971. "Belief in the Law of Small Numbers." *Psychological Bulletin* 80, pp. 352–373.

Tversky, A., and D. Kahneman. 1974. "Judgment Under Uncertainty: Heuristics and Biases." *Science* 185, pp. 1124–1131.

Tversky, A., and D. Kahneman. 1981. "The Framing of Decisions and the Psychology of Choice." *Science* 211, pp. 453–458.

Tversky, A., and D. Kahneman. 1983. "Extension Versus Intuitive Reasoning: The Conjunctive Fallacy in Probability Judgment." *Psychological Review* 90, no. 4, pp. 293–315.

Ulich, E., and W.G. Weber. 1996. "Dimensions, Criteria, and Evaluation Of Work Group Autonomy.". In *Handbook of Work Group Psychology*, ed. M.A. West, 249–282. Chichester, UK: Wiley.

Van Rooy, D.L., and C. Viswesvaran. 2004. "Emotional Intelligence: A Meta-Analytic Investigation of Predictive Validity and Nomological net." *Journal of Vocational Behavior* 65, no. 1, pp. 71–95.

Vicere, A.A., and R.M. Fulmer. 1997. *Leadership by Design*. Boston, MA: Harvard Business School Press.

Viswesvaran, C., J.I. Sanchez, and J. Fisher. 1999. "The Role of Social Support in the Process of Work Stress: A Meta-Analysis." *Journal of Vocational Behavior* 54, no. 2, pp. 314–334.

VitalSmarts. 2009. *Long-Distance Loathing (Summary and Data)*. Provo, UT: VitalSmarts.

Vroom, V.H. 1964. *Work and Motivation*. New York: Wiley.

Waldeck, J.H., and Myers, K.K. 2008. "Organizational Assimilation Theory, Research, and Implications for Multiple Areas of the Discipline: A State of the Art Review." In *Communication Yearbook*, ed. C.S. Beck, 31, 322–367. New York, NY: Lawrence Erlbaum.

Walter, F., R.H. Humphrey, and M.S. Cole. 2012. "Unleashing Leadership Potential: Toward An Evidence-Based Management of Emotional Intelligence." *Organizational Dynamics* 41, pp. 212–219.

Wanous, J.P. 1992. *Organizational Entry: Recruitment, Selection, Orientation and Socialization of Newcomers*. Reading, MA: Addison-Wesley.

Ward, C., R. Fischer, F.S. Zaid Lam, and L. Hall. 2009. "The Convergent, Discriminant, and Incremental Validity of Scores on a Self-Report Measure of Cultural Intelligence." *Educational and Psychological Measurement* 69, no. 1, pp. 85–105.

Wason, P.C. 1968. "Reasoning About a Rule." *Quarterly Journal of Experimental Psychology* 20, pp. 273–281.

Wechsler, D. 1939. *The Measurement of Adult Intelligence*. Baltimore, MD: Williams & Wilkins.

Weick, K.E. 1995. Sense-making in Organizations. Thousand Oaks, CA: Sage.

Wellbourne, T., and M. Andrews. 1996. "Predicting Performance of IPOs: Should Human Resource Management be in the Equation?" *Academy of Management Journal* 39, pp. 891–919.

Whetton, D. A., and K.S. Cameron. 2011. *Developing Management Skills*, 8th ed. Upper Saddle River, NJ: Prentice-Hall.

World at Work. February, 2009. *Telework Trendlines*. Scottsdale, AZ: World at Work.

Zaccaro, S.A., R.J. Foti, and D.A. Kenny. 1991. "Self-monitoring and Trait-Based Variance in Leadership: An Investigation of Leader Flexibility Across Multiple Group Situations." *Journal of Applied Psychology* 76, no. 2, pp. 308–315.

Zachary, L.J. 2000. *The Mentor's Guide: Facilitating Effective Learning Relationships*. San Francisco. CA: Jossey-Bass.

Zhang, D.C., and S. Highhouse. 2018. "Judgment and Decision Making in the Workplace." In *The SAGE Handbook of Industrial, Work, & Organizational Psychology and Employee Performance*, eds. D.S. Ones, N. Anderson, C. Viswesvaran, H.K. Sinangli, 611–633. Thousand Oaks, CA: Sage.

About the Author

Dean E. Frost is Professor of Business Administration at Bemidji State University, one of the seven Minnesota State University campus locations. Formerly, he was a faculty member at the University of Virginia, Duquesne University, Portland State University, and Walden University. At Bemidji State University, Dr. Frost teaches Strategic Management, Business Analytics, Labor and Employment Relations, International Management, and Organizational Behavior.

Dr. Frost has published scholarly work in such fields as Implicit Leadership Theory, Management Development, Emotional Intelligence, Occupational Health Psychology, Financial Decision Making, Social Power, and the Prediction of Leadership Effectiveness. He has worked on projects for such organizations as Federal Emergency Management Agency, the Defense Advanced Research Projects Agency, the Seattle Fire Department, Oregon Saw Chain, Intel, Johnstone Supply, Crown Zellerbach, Newhouse Publications, and the National Institute for Occupational Safety and Health.

His credentials include a bachelor's degree from Reed College, and a master's and doctoral degree from the University of Washington. He has been a member of the Academy of Management for 40 years. He has served on over 50 thesis and dissertation committees over the years and has over 25 publications, including the book *Strategic Management* (2021).

Index

OTHER TITLES IN THE HUMAN RESOURCE MANAGEMENT AND ORGANIZATIONAL BEHAVIOR COLLECTION

Michael Provitera, Barry University, Editor

- *A.I. and Remote Working* by Tony Miller
- *Best Boss!* by Duncan Ferguson, Toni M. Pristo, and John Furcon
- *Managing for Accountability* by Lynne Curry
- *Emotional Connection: The EmC Strategy* by Lola Gershfeld and Ramin Sedehi
- *Fundamentals of Level Three Leadership* by James G.S. Clawson
- *Civility at Work* by Lewena Bayer
- *Lean on Civility* by Christian Masotti and Lewena Bayer
- *Leaderocity* by Richard Dool
- *Agility* by Michael Edmondson
- *Strengths Oriented Leadership* by Matt L. Beadle
- *Leadership In Disruptive Times* by Sattar Bawany
- *The Successful New CEO* by Christian Muntean

Concise and Applied Business Books

The Collection listed above is one of 30 business subject collections that Business Expert Press has grown to make BEP a premiere publisher of print and digital books. Our concise and applied books are for...

- Professionals and Practitioners
- Faculty who adopt our books for courses
- Librarians who know that BEP's Digital Libraries are a unique way to offer students ebooks to download, not restricted with any digital rights management
- Executive Training Course Leaders
- Business Seminar Organizers

Business Expert Press books are for anyone who needs to dig deeper on business ideas, goals, and solutions to everyday problems. Whether one print book, one ebook, or buying a digital library of 110 ebooks, we remain the affordable and smart way to be business smart. For more information, please visit www.businessexpertpress.com, or contact sales@businessexpertpress.com.

www.ingramcontent.com/pod-product-compliance
Lightning Source LLC
Chambersburg PA
CBHW061216220326
41599CB00025B/4655